Dear
Jesus is new 'dr your 'Life House'. A whole new wardrobe awaits. Enjoy my friend Enjoy!

RESTORE YOUR LIFE

How God renovates us from the inside out

love + kisses
Mindy x

Revelation 19:6-9

Mandy Muckett

Copyright © 2022–Mandy Muckett

All rights reserved. This book is protected under the copyright laws. This book may not be copied or reprinted for commercial gain or profit. The use of short quotations or occasional page copying for personal or group study is permitted. Permission can be obtained upon written request from Mandy Muckett.

While all the stories in this book are true, some names and identifying information in this book have been changed to protect the privacy of the individuals involved.

All Scripture quotations, unless otherwise noted, taken from the Holy Bible, New International Version®, NIV®. Copyright © 1973, 1978, 1984, 2011 by Biblica, Inc.™ Used by permission of Zondervan. All rights reserved worldwide www.zondervan.com The "NIV" and "New International Version" are trademarks registered in the United States Patent and Trademark Office by Biblica, Inc.™

Scripture quotations are also taken from the Amplified® Bible, AMP. Copyright © 2015 by The Lockman Foundation. Used by permission. www.lockman.org

Scripture quotations are also taken from THE MESSAGE, MSG. Copyright © 1993, 1994, 1995, 1996, 2000, 2001, 2002 by Eugene H. Peterson. Used by permission of NavPress. All rights reserved. Represented by Tyndale House Publishers, Inc.

All emphasis within Scripture is the author's own. Please also note that the publishing style does not capitalise the name of satan and related names. Choosing not to acknowledge him, even to the point of violating grammatical rules.

This and other books by Mandy Muckett are available at Christian bookshops and distributors worldwide.

For any other correspondence:
Email: info@mandymuckett.com

Internet: www.mandymuckett.com

Book cover design: Obed & Shalomie Tewes, TewesCo
http://www.tewesco.com

Book interior design: Polgarus Studio
www.polgarusstudio.com

Author's picture - back cover: Veronica Kiefer Photography
www.veronicakiefer.com

Author's picture - Styling: Loreta Schöpfer
Hairstyle & Face, Arlesheim, Switzerland.

ISBN 978-3-9523254-2-1
ISBN EBOOK 978-3-9523254-3-8

Dedication

This book is dedicated to Jesus, my saviour, my king and my friend, who has transformed my life beyond all imaginings.

Come and hear, all you who fear God;
let me tell you what he has done for me.
Psalm 66:16

PRAISE FOR *RESTORE YOUR LIFE*

Lora Allison
Written in a warm and delightful style, Mandy has provided us with an adventure in living! She has a refreshing way of teaching us to live a full and deep life with the Lord in our practical everyday experiences. One of my favourite parts is the chapter on love. All of us desire love, and even desire to give love; however sometimes it seems to grow more complicated the more we look for it. Mandy encourages us that we must love both ourselves and others but with the love of God. And therein lies the adventure, a real-life adventure in love! I encourage you to experience this restoration in your own life in *Restore Your Life!*

Lora Allison, founder of Celebration Ministries, travels and teaches in many nations and is the author of seven books. Her latest, *Kingdom Alignment*, is available on Amazon.

www.celebrationministries.com.

Paul Harcourt
One of the foundational truths of the gospel is that God loves everything that he has made, and never gives up on us. Mandy writes in a really helpful way, with a sweetness and simplicity borne of deep personal experience, about our great God - the master Restorer!

Paul Harcourt, National leader of New Wine England and Vicar of All Saints, Woodford Wells, London, England

www.new-wine.org

Allen Hood

Every human being deserves a place to call home. Journey with Mandy through the pages of *Restore your Life* to discover the home Jesus has in mind for you. Repairing what is broken. Renovating your 'Life House', room by room. Restoring you, His dwelling place and calling you home.

Allen Hood – Former Associate Director of the IHOPKC Missions Base and Executive Pastor of Forerunner Church, International House of Prayer Kansas City, USA
www.allenhood.com
www.ihopkc.org

Julie Meyer

Mandy is an amazing writer who will speak directly to your heart, speak truth and in the very same breath, you will see yourself and smile. She writes from such a personal place that each reader will be able to identify with. Read along as Mandy shares personal stories of encouragement and break through. You will experience the same as you read *'Restore Your Life'*.

Julie Meyer – Worship leader, songwriter, author and international speaker
Healing Rooms Apostolic Centre, Santa Maria, USA
www.juliemeyerministries.com

Christian Willi

In her very inspiring new book *Restore your Life*, Mandy gives a touching description of her visit to Kenya seeing firsthand the work of Compassion in the field. Mandy has been advocating on behalf of children living in poverty for years and her heart for the poor and for the neighbor more generally shows how purposeful our life can become.

Christian Willi – CEO Compassion Schweiz
www.Compassion.ch

ACKNOWLEDGEMENTS

To my ever-patient husband Keith who, without complaint, laid aside our time together on holiday so I could concentrate on writing. I couldn't have completed this project without your continual encouragement and professional project management skills– thank you darling.

To Clare Rogers, your discerning editorial insight and professional touch have guided and stretched my writing to a deeper and richer place, and I am forever in your debt.

To Shalomie Tewes, who came as a gift to me from God. You were God's fulfilment of the prophetic dream for this book. You have supported and encouraged me during not only its birthing process but so much more too. You'll never know just how grateful I am.

To Veronica Kiefer and Loreta Schöpfer, my beautiful and talented girlfriends. Thank you both for making me look even more *Gorgeous!*

To the numerous waiting staff in Aptos, the Black Forest, Barcelona, Madrid, and Milan who supplied me with coffee – your service with a smile kept me going in those long hours of writing.

And last but by no means least, to my dearest friends Steve and Helen Judkins – thank you for the use of your apartment in Paphos. That view of the Mediterranean was a true inspiration.

Contents

INTRODUCTION 11
CHAPTER 1 – MAKING A HOUSE A HOME 12
CHAPTER 2 – KNOCK, KNOCK, WHO'S THERE? 18
CHAPTER 3 – ENTER THE KING 27
CHAPTER 4 – BUILT ON THE ROCK 39
CHAPTER 5 – UP ON THE ROOF 48
CHAPTER 6 – THE HEART OF THE HOME 58
CHAPTER 7 – COME DINE WITH ME 69
CHAPTER 8 – ROOM FOR ALL THE FAMILY 81
CHAPTER 9 – AND NOW DOWN TO BUSINESS 92
CHAPTER 10 – BOUDOIRS AND BUBBLE BATHS 105
CHAPTER 11 – LET'S GET PHYSICAL! 118
CHAPTER 12 – WHAT ARE YOU LOOKING AT? 130
CHAPTER 13 – STORAGE HOARDERS 141
CHAPTER 14 – HOME AWAY FROM HOME 154
CHAPTER 15 – OUR HEAVENLY HOME 165
APPENDIX – INVITING JESUS 175
AFTERWORD 177
ABOUT THE AUTHOR 179

INTRODUCTION

Hello! I'm Mandy – pleased to meet you.

Thank you for picking up this book. I'm wondering what drew you to a title like *Restore your Life*. Are you one of those random browsers whose interest is caught by a book cover, or are you a 'doer', searching for the next project? Perhaps you are an explorer, willing to journey into the unknown in search of yourself and more of God?

Well, we may have something in common, because I am all the above. Learning new things can be a bit daunting, especially if you feel alone in your need of improvement. So, do you fancy a companion on this journey of discovery? I've been on the road called 'faith' for a little while now. I'm no expert, but I can tell you some things I've learnt along the way, and perhaps I can encourage you too as we journey together, seeking to become more than we currently are by delving into the depths of God.

I think this sums it up nicely:

> Now the Lord is the Spirit, and where the Spirit of the Lord is, there is freedom. And we all, who with unveiled faces contemplate the Lord's glory, are being transformed into his image with ever-increasing glory, which comes from the Lord, who is the Spirit.
>
> 2 Corinthians 3:17–18

CHAPTER 1
MAKING A HOUSE A HOME

I am one of those people who are fascinated by houses. My dreams are, more often than not, filled with them – in all shapes, sizes and states of repair. I love whiling away an hour or so watching shows about them on TV, whether it's 'Fixer Upper', 'Homes under the Hammer', 'Grand Designs', 'Changing Rooms' or, dare I say it, 'Through the Keyhole', I enjoy looking inside other people's houses. From a wreck won at auction and fully restored, via designer architect plans brought to life or room transformations in under a day, to just an old-fashioned nose around someone else's house, I am enthralled. I also love looking at people's houses as I walk my dog Benson, and often wonder what sort of people live inside.

Ideal home

I guess it stems from my childhood. As well as my love of playing with my dolls' house, I have great memories of an annual pilgrimage to London from the age of about five, to visit the Ideal Home Show along with three generations of my family.[1] If you've never heard of it, the Ideal Home Show is an institution on the UK exhibition calendar. Every year since 1908, for a couple of weeks in the spring, London's Earls Court has been transformed into a mecca for those seeking home improvement. It brings to the masses the latest designs and inventions that could make your home 'ideal'.

You may think it strange that a child enjoyed such a day out. For many

---

[1] See its history here: www.idealhomeshow.co.uk/visiting/ideal-home-show-history

children it would be an endurance test – a long, boring hike, with the adults in the family seemingly stopping every five minutes to look at stands overflowing with stuff of no relevance to a child at all. But looking back now, I think I was unusual in that I really enjoyed all the exhibits and demonstrations. In fact, it was good that I went when I did, because as an adult I would be tempted to buy every single new-fangled gadget on display. I'd want the newest way to chop a carrot or get my windows to gleam that little bit brighter. How could I not need to purchase the latest gadget? My life would be empty without it, right?

During the 70s, 80s and 90s, the exhibition became famous for building actual villages of new houses as a showcase for the building trade. This was my highlight – even if we had to queue for what felt like hours. For me it was like walking into wonderland; my version of a Santa's grotto. Through every door and around every corner there were delights to find: perfect kitchens with dazzling worktops; elegant dining rooms with crystal chandeliers and bone china; luxurious bathrooms with sunken whirlpools; and sweeping staircases that could take me to heaven. Wow, this was the life! This was what I aspired to when I grew up and had a house of my own.

It was not until decades later that I began to learn a valuable lesson. It is said that things are not always what they seem, and the perfect show houses I remember are a brilliant example of this: what was portrayed on the outside was not the reality underneath. I suppose, as children do, I took everything at face value. I did not question what my eyes told me. What I did not know then, but know now, was that those gorgeous dreams for sale *were not real.* The street of houses that filled me with awe as a child was in fact a collection of fabricated shells. They were replicas of the real, like movie sets. The appliances had no plumbing and the wall sockets no power. The sumptuous pillows and duvets covered a collection of packing boxes masquerading as king-size beds, and even the loaf that graced the bread board in the kitchen was plastic. It was a sterile environment – deceptively perfect houses like those on the sets of 'Desperate Housewives' or 'The Truman Show'.

They were created for one purpose, consumerism – that never ending black hole of accumulating stuff, forever empty, always wanting more, never being satisfied in the search for completeness. These soulless places were created to sell us an empty version of a reality that would devour our energy, waste our time, demand our focus, divert our purpose and ultimately destroy the lives we were really created to live. Oh, what a disappointment, all those aspirations, just a representation, not the real thing at all! Now I'm all grown up and have experienced some of what the human existence involves, I have come to see through this industry that sells us the dream of the ultimate lifestyle – with all the materialistic clobber we're supposed to buy to attain it.

I wonder if you dream of an ideal home – or if you have a dream for your life. As with the fantasy of the perfect house, we all long for our lives to be more than they currently are. Often, we want the lives other people live instead of our own, full of longing to have what we do not, striving to be more but never reaching our full potential.

I want to invite you, through the pages of this book, to use the idea of a house as an analogy for your life. If you are anything like me, you'll agree that the reality of life doesn't always live up to the ideal of our hearts. If my life were a house, I can tell you there have been times in the past when I longed to demolish the whole thing and start again. But I was invited into a gradual process of transformation, one that would turn my wreck into a vibrant home, full of life, light and love; and this book is my invitation to you, to journey with me along the path to restoration.

How to use this book

My own process of transformation began after I found faith in God, many years ago as a young mother, and much of it came through learning to listen to him. I'd stumbled across a very effective way of letting him speak to me quite early on. This is what I do: I picture a scene in my 'mind's eye' – in other words my imagination – and I invite the Holy Spirit to let the scene unfold as he wants it to. What happens then has often and unexpectedly revealed powerful truths to me, sometimes in words, mostly pictures, sometimes both. An important part of the process for me is 'journaling' – writing down (or even drawing) the images and words I receive in my journal.

It was through listening to God in this way that I wrote this book.

"Use your imagination? That's just making things up!" you might say. And it's true that when a picture comes to mind in prayer, it might be 'just you', or God, or a combination of the two. But the fact that your imagination is involved doesn't mean you're making it up. Our mind's eye is a powerful tool that God has used to communicate with us from the time of the Old Testament prophets to the modern day, via St Ignatius and his famous 'spiritual exercises'.

So, I invite you to do the same as you read this book. There are 'restoration reflections' at the end of each chapter to guide you. Practically speaking, all you need is some time on your own, a Bible, and a pen and notebook so you can write it down afterwards. Ask the Holy Spirit to guide your imagination, then picture the scene suggested in the reflection; such as your life as a house, or a conversation with God about one of its rooms. And let the Holy Spirit, through your imagination, take you where he will. Don't try to work out at this point whether it's God or not – just go with the flow. You can evaluate later. When you've finished, write down what came to mind, and see if it holds any significance for you.

House or home?

When you think of the difference between a house and a home what comes to mind? For me, it's an old soul song by Dionne Warwick: 'A house is not a home'.[2] The lyrics tell us that the difference is not only life, but love. Humans can reside in a building and not make it a home. A home is created when love dwells there. And its square footage is ultimately irrelevant: a little wooden shack filled with love is a palace, compared to a mansion filled with hate and loathing, quiet indifference or unspoken despair.

As a house without love is not a home, there is something else that makes our 'life houses' empty. It's not something that can be seen on the outside. Outwardly your life may have all the trappings of success: satisfying career,

---

[2] Dionne Warwick (1964) 'A house is not a home', Scepter Records. Song originally written by Burt Bacharach and Hal David

holidays, hobbies; even helping others and the love of family and friends. But there is another perspective: God's. "The Lord does not look at the things people look at. People look at the outward appearance, but the Lord looks at the heart" (1 Sam 16:7). No matter how we portray ourselves to the outside world or even to those closest to us, God sees our innermost being. And from his perspective, our lives are incomplete outside a loving relationship with him.

So, if a house truly becomes a home when it has love in it, and if we use the metaphor of a house to represent your life, is your 'life house' alive in love? God is love! So God is fulfilling his part of the relationship – how are you doing? Is your relationship with God alive or just a religious practice? More importantly – are you in relationship with him at all? Even the best this world can offer pales into insignificance compared to the full, vibrant life God offers us in relationship with him. The big question is: Do you know how to find it?

RESTORATION REFLECTION

What does your 'ideal home' look like, in your mind's eye? Is it an imperial palace – a cosy thatched cottage – a canal boat?

- Take a moment with your eyes closed to picture your ideal home – let your imagination run wild!

- Now try to picture your own life as a house. Start at the front door and look into every room. What comes to mind?

The second exercise might be difficult – perhaps you think your life/house isn't 'good enough' or falls far below your own ideal. On the other hand, maybe you'll 'see' good things about it that you hadn't noticed before. Either way, I can assure you that God sees the beauty in your life – the life he created – beneath any blemishes. His purpose is not to find fault, but to help you become who you were always intended to be. My prayer is that this book will help you on that journey.

CHAPTER 2
KNOCK, KNOCK, WHO'S THERE?

Homelessness is awful. I can't begin to imagine what it would be like for me and my family. But for millions of people, it is their daily reality.

We are homeless

There are many reasons for homelessness, and poverty is one of the greatest. Jesus said "the poor will always be with you" (Mark 14:7) and that is as true today as it was in his time. Tens of millions of people are homeless due to poverty. Then there is the homelessness caused by the terror of war, when people flee their homes in fear for their lives – often to be herded into squalid tented camps, or left out, completely exposed, in the worst weather. Homeless people are subjected not only to the elements and lack of food, but preyed on by the evil of people traffickers who seek out the most vulnerable to enslave and sell on for their own ill-gotten gain.

Another homelessness crisis was caused in 2008 by what has been coined the 'subprime mortgage crisis'. The onset of a severe global recession saw foreclosures of mortgages leading to people in the West, especially in America, having their houses repossessed by banks. It's sobering to imagine the panic and fear of hearing that dreaded knock, only for the door to be opened to a person serving you with an eviction notice. Or to imagine those families who once had a roof over their heads now out on the street with nowhere to go, lives devastated for generations to come. To be evicted or have to flee from your home must be high up on the list of the most painful and stressful things a person can go through in life.

When you see a figure huddled in a sleeping bag on the pavement, it's obvious that this person is homeless; but homelessness goes far beyond what you can see. Homelessness is more than just having nowhere to sleep or eat or not having a tenancy or a mortgage. It is a state of being invisible, a sense of insecurity and helplessness – no longer being a person, but just a statistic of a broken society.

Yet, those who have a roof over their heads can be homeless too. Eviction from our homes is not a new phenomenon for human beings. History itself had an eviction at its start, with the story of Adam and Eve. Where once humans walked with God in the Garden of Eden, wrong choices led to the first case of homelessness. Where once we found our home with God, sin brought separation and death. Homelessness at its most profound, then, is a state of being out of relationship with God. Since that first eviction, we have tried time and time again to get back 'home'. This is why, even if everything in our lives seems to be okay, we can feel a deep ache of emptiness and unfulfilled longing. Our soul knows it is homeless, even if our minds do not. We've sought to undo the eviction notice served on all of humanity – by means of self-improvement.

Alone, we can do much to improve ourselves. We can care for our physical bodies. We can train our mind, emotions and will. But the Bible gives us a warning: 'There is a way that seems right to a man, but in the end it leads to death' (Prov 14:12). The choice Adam and Eve made, after listening to that darn snake in the garden, may have seemed right to them at the time – but it led to their separation from God and ultimately to physical death. And that's the tragedy of death: it goes hand in hand with separation, tearing us apart from those we love.

Coming home

That first case of homelessness is echoed in the famous story of the prodigal son (Luke 15: 11–31). It tells of a father and two sons. One of them leaves home, wanting to go his own way – but ultimately ends up close to death before deciding to return home. The bit I especially love in this story is the response of the father to the sight of his son coming home: "But while he was still a long way off, his father saw him and was filled with compassion for him; he ran to his son, threw his arms around him and kissed him".

Yes, this is a loving father who allowed his child free choice; but despite the son's failure, runs out to welcome him home with a loving embrace. A true homecoming indeed!

Man-made religion, obeying laws and doing 'good works' are some of the ways we try to improve ourselves, thinking that if we only try harder we can restore the relationship with God that has been lost. Does this resonate with you? Will you ever feel good enough to be accepted 'home' again? But we humans are separated from God, not just in body and soul, but spiritually. And if we are spiritually separated from God – spiritually dead so to speak – what hope do we have? Just doing good things will not be enough. The question is then, how do we get 'home'?

Back in the time of Jesus, a man called Nicodemus was asking the same question (John 3:1–21). Jesus told Nicodemus that a man had to be 'born again'. A spiritual rebirth is needed. Adhering to a religion cannot bring about a rebirth, no matter how hard we try. The Bible tells us that to 'be saved' – or in other words, be restored to our original love relationship with God – we need to have faith in the person and work of Jesus Christ.

In our self-sufficient world, the word 'faith' is often derided. Faith is for the wacky. Faith is for the weak. Isn't faith in Jesus a crutch for people who are unable to control their emotions or circumstances by sheer will alone? However, the reality is that the people whose weaknesses are obvious, and who have come to the end of their personal abilities, are likely to be much closer to spiritual rebirth than those who are seemingly strong. When we come to 'the end of ourselves' we open the door to realising that we weren't created to be independent, solitary beings at all, but a people who were made to live depending on a relationship with the God who loves us unconditionally. This human weakness is not only encouraged; it is called 'blessed' in the Bible. In his famous 'sermon on the mount', Jesus said "Blessed are the poor [weak] in spirit, for theirs is the kingdom of heaven" (Matt 5:3). Acknowledging we need God is a blessing, one that is essential to the renovation process. It is interesting to add that hardship and suffering can lead many to seek, through recognition of their own human weakness, connection on a spiritual level with God. Often it appears that the fastest-growing numbers of vibrant believers in Jesus are in parts of the world that experience the highest levels of conflict, violence and persecution.

The storm of God's love

At this point I'd like to share a personal experience with you. As I said in my introduction, I want to be your companion on this journey to 'restore your life' – and as part of our walk together I want to be as open and honest with you as I can. My aim is that you don't feel alone, or that you are the only person who needs 'fixing'!

In my own journey of discovery, I have found it helpful to listen to God in the way I described in the last chapter, writing my prayers in a journal together with the answers I receive. It's often how I speak to God, and have been doing this now for many years. It was while listening to God and journaling one morning, sitting under the pergola in our garden, that God spoke to me about this very issue of being separated from him. As I prayed and wrote, a picture came into my mind of an old-fashioned fairground, with various rides and stalls representing different aspects of sin in my life. Jesus and I walked around the fair, and suffice to say that my sin wasn't very pretty to behold. He showed me, among other things, how I run away from him to climb the 'helter-skelter' of pride (see Chapter 5).

Then something happened during my journaling session that interrupted my writing. Here's how I described it in my journal:

> 18 December 2000
> *The weather has changed while I have been writing in the garden. A sudden storm has appeared from nowhere. A heavy downpour of rain. The weight of the massive rain drops picturing for me the tears that roll down Jesus' face, as he sees me turn away from him time and time again, choosing my way instead of his. The sun is obscured by gigantic*

black clouds. The first clap of thunder crashes overhead. I'm deafened by hail that now hammers on the roof of the pergola above me. It is like an awful encounter with a raging yet loving God who hates sin – but in his supreme love for me allows my free will. Should I retreat into the house or stay and experience the storm? I decide to stay. The deluge of water is now spraying me as I write, like the blood of Christ's sacrifice washing away my sin, judging all sin as God did in the time of Noah. Lightning stabs the sky! I cower from the strength of the storm, God's wrath, his righteous anger, his awesome power, his sovereign will. The hail stones are like cannon balls raining down a heavenly assault, like a war of love, a battle in the spirit realm. I begin to cry. I cry hard hot tears that streak my cheeks. I feel as if I will never stop crying. My wailing is drowned out by the torrent of sound made by the storm. I close my eyes in a futile attempt to escape. I wait. When I dare to open my eyes, I realise that I'm not swept away, even though the storm still rages all around me. I'm protected by my Lord, the canopy of his love covering the multitude of my sins.

You may be thinking that I'm making a big deal out of a simple thunder storm. But to me it was a graphic demonstration that yes, God hates sin, but he doesn't hate me! God is not tolerant where sin is concerned. The strength of the storm gave me a faint idea or echo of just how great the wrath of God will be when sin is judged. It's God's love and justice that causes him to hate sin – his concern for the weak and those sinned against means that judge it he must. God hates sin; but he loves you. In fact, he is crazy about you, so much so that he had a plan in action to restore you to himself even while you were still sinning.

I just love this from the Message Bible:

> It wasn't so long ago that you were mired in that old stagnant life of sin. You let the world, which doesn't know the first thing about living, tell you how to live. You filled your lungs with polluted unbelief, and then exhaled disobedience. We all did it, all of us

doing what we felt like doing, when we felt like doing it, all of us in the same boat. It's a wonder God didn't lose his temper and do away with the whole lot of us. Instead, immense in mercy and with an incredible love, he embraced us. He took our sin-dead lives and made us alive in Christ. He did all this on his own, with no help from us! Then he picked us up and set us down in highest heaven in company with Jesus, our Messiah.

Ephesians 2:1–5 (MSG)

The Restoration Man

So then – how can the house of our life be restored? God is the architect. He has, and has always had, the plan to restore us to our former glory, in loving relationship with himself. With God as architect, this will be a perfectly professional restoration. Let's not try to do some amateur DIY job, because any attempts to change through our own good works are utterly worthless.

No matter how unsavoury we may think his methods, God's plan is to bring us back into relationship with him, in all his perfection, on a bloodied wooden cross. And not only did Jesus pay the price for our sin through his own death and separation from Father God – his resurrection offers us eternal restoration:

> …anyone united with the Messiah gets a fresh start, is created new. The old life is gone; a new life burgeons! Look at it! All this comes from the God who settled the relationship between us and him, and then called us to settle our relationships with each other. God put the world square with himself through the Messiah, giving the world a fresh start by offering forgiveness of sins.
>
> 2 Corinthians 5:17–19a (MSG)

The question is – do you *want* to be made new? If you have never put your trust in Christ before, he can make you new. If you have taken this step before but wandered off, however far, however often, he can make you new.

However old you are and however stuck in your habits, he can make you new. But it's *your choice*.

There are no forced makeovers. It is impossible to be forcibly converted to faith in Jesus (or reconverted, for those of us who wandered off). It is a matter of free will, your free choice, a heart matter. Just like falling in love, you can't be forced into loving someone. Salvation, like love, is a mystery. We can try to understand how it works but all that's needed, when all is said and done, is our heart's agreement – a simple step of faith to believe in the Restoration Man, Jesus.

One famous painting is loved by preachers: Light of the World by William Holman Hunt.[3] It has been used countless times as a sermon illustration because it shows Jesus knocking on an overgrown and long unopened door – with no handle on the outside. The door can only be opened from the inside. The same is true of our life houses. Is the door to the house of your life like the one in Hunt's picture, overgrown with weeds and long unopened? Jesus can knock but he can't, and would never, open the door for you. It is your choice. Do you hear him knocking and will you let him in?

If you choose to open that door, remember, this is no game of 'Knock Down Ginger'. Jesus does not knock on your door then run away and hide! He will never leave you standing alone if you open your life to him. So, take down the guard around the door to your heart, unlatch the safety chain, and let his eternal love into your life.[4] Once you do, you will discover that not only does Jesus want to be with you, he wants to live in and through you. Let's take the next steps together and see what he will do to restore the house of your life.

---

[3] William Holman Hunt, 'The Light of the World', painted 1853/4
[4] There is a prayer to help you do this in the appendix at the end of the book

RESTORATION REFLECTION

Choose one of the scenes below, then close your eyes and ask God to guide your imagination as you picture it. You might find it helpful to write down or draw what you saw in your mind's eye afterwards.

- Imagine you are on your way home to Father God after a long time away. Picture the house a little way off down the road, and the father starting to come towards you with open arms.

    How do you feel – is it easy or hard to run into his embrace? What does he say to you and what do you say to him? Do you feel welcome? How does it feel to step through the front door?

- You are just inside your own front door and you hear knocking. You know that it's Jesus on the other side, gently asking to come in.

    How do you feel – is it scary or exciting to think he's right there on the other side of the door? Do you want to fling the door open, or bolt it shut and walk away? Is there anything you might say to him, or him to you, through the letterbox? What happens if you open the door?

TALK TO THE ARCHITECT

Lord Jesus I have opened the door to you, the only one who can restore my life. Please be welcome in me. I'm sorry that in the past I ignored you or refused your help – please forgive me. Show me where you were in my life when I have been, or felt, homeless. Please work in me and restore every area of my life as you see fit. Amen.

CHAPTER 3
ENTER THE KING

Perhaps you have already opened the front door of your 'life house' to Jesus. You may not have had the red carpet out or a brass band playing, but how you go about welcoming Jesus is not what's important here. For some, taking a step of faith in the person and work of Jesus Christ is an overwhelming, explosive life event – whereas for others, it is a quiet 'Yes', spoken by a heart over a period of time. The *way* of accepting Jesus is irrelevant compared to *who* you have opened your life to. If you have let him in, do you realise that you've invited royalty inside?

Who's got the power?

I am English, and in the United Kingdom we know quite a bit about royalty. Our Queen is known worldwide; she is now the longest serving monarch in the UK's history. I can only imagine how I would react if I had Queen Elizabeth II standing in my hallway! (Woah, have I dusted and cleaned? Have I hidden all my mess away where it can't be seen?) How do you think you would feel standing in such company? Would you curtsey or bow, or even kneel?

People from the UK are familiar with royalty in a way that people from other nations may not be; the continued existence of the aristocracy make words like duke, earl, and baron part of our vocabulary. And whether we love them or hate them, we are interested in the royal family. Their words and actions regularly fill our TV screens or news headlines. But what real influence do they have on our everyday lives? No matter how rooted these titles are in the British psyche, the meaning and authority behind such positions has long since diminished. Queen Elizabeth II no longer holds the power that the monarchy held historically. She is a figurehead for her country, carrying out ceremonial duties, and although the words of the national anthem declare "long to reign over us" she holds no power to reign or rule over anyone. Our elected government now holds the power (which is just as well, given that kings and queens of old tended to chop off the heads of those who displeased them).

So, now that the modern monarchy has lost its power to strike fear and awe into our hearts, what is our understanding of the title given to Jesus? If we are to believe that Jesus is, as the Bible calls him, King of kings and Lord of lords – how then are we to behave in his presence? Jesus said, "My kingdom is not of this world" (John 18:36). If Jesus is the king of more than just an earthly kingdom, the Kings of *all* kings and Lord of *all* lords, shouldn't we at least kneel before him?

The word 'lord' is rarely used these days outside Christian prayer, but when it is, it's often used in the phrase 'lording it over someone'. Historically the 'Lord of the Manor' owned not only the land that he held by title deed, but he also held power over the people that inhabited and worked that land. This kind of lordship was often cruel, treating people little better than animals. But godly lordship is something different altogether, and I want to invite you through the rest of this chapter to explore the lordship Jesus brings with him when he comes to live in the house of your life.

The carpenter king

Picture the scene: Jesus is here, standing in the hallway of your life house. Are you standing there open-mouthed, or lying prostrate on the floor? Either way, I want to suggest that you look at Jesus, really look at his face, in your 'mind's eye'. You may be surprised at what you see.

Yes, Jesus is the one who sits at the right hand of God the Father in heaven – but he is also a craftsman, not unused to hard work – a carpenter. He stands before you with his sleeves rolled up, ready to start on your restoration. Jesus is the 'servant king' who said of himself, "…the Son of Man came not to be waited on, but to serve" (Matt 20:28a). He is not an earthly dictator who rules by force, violence and oppression; neither is he the ruler of some kind of nanny state, nagging you into submission. No, he is the man with the plan. "For I know the plans I have for you," declares the LORD, "plans to prosper you and not to harm you, plans to give you hope and a future" (Jer 29:11). Not only did God have the plan to save us by restoring our relationship with himself, he also has a plan to transform us. It is the process we go through to become the person God created us to be, a reflection of Jesus himself.

Can you see Jesus the carpenter in your mind's eye? For a helpful picture of God as carpenter, and us as his handiwork, I recommend a children's picture book by Max Lucado called *You are Special*.[5] It is one of my favourites. (I hope you're not offended that I suggest reading a children's story– but if Jesus can speak to me through a children's book, then why not anyone?)

The story centres on a community of little wooden people called 'Wemmicks' who spend their lives giving each other stickers – either grey spot stickers to the scratched, chipped or generally broken Wemmicks, or golden star stickers to the popular, talented, beautiful Wemmicks. The central character, Punchenello, is one of those Wemmicks who gets covered in grey spots. He meets a Wemmick by the name of Lucia who's unusual because she has neither spots nor stars. She tells him that none of them will stick to her, because she often visits Eli, the woodcarver and creator of all the Wemmicks. Punchenello then goes to see him.

The picture of the character Eli in the book is one of a rough and ready but kindly carpenter, who clearly loves his creations. After a short conversation with Eli, one of Punchenello's grey spots begins to peel off. What mattered was not the opinions of the other Wemmicks, but the love and acceptance of the one who had made him.

Jesus, having trained as a carpenter, knows how to look at a big old hunk of wood and see a beautiful masterpiece hidden in the depths of the grain. In

---

[5] Max Lucado (1997) *You are Special*, Crossway Books

the same way, Jesus can see who we *really are*, despite the mess our lives currently display. What matters is what God thinks and feels about us. We can try to put on a show, make a good impression and present to others what we think they want to see, but the reality is that Jesus sees us as we truly are – there is nowhere to hide. 'Is there any place I can go to avoid your Spirit? …If I flew on morning's wings to the far western horizon, you'd find me in a minute—you're already there waiting! (Ps 139:7–10 MSG).

As I've got older I've come to realise that in the whole scheme of things, it doesn't matter what other people think of me. Jesus taught me this lesson using my home in Switzerland as an example. Our house was built in the 1970s and needs a lot of renovation. A friend of ours suggested we take advice from an interior decorator they had previously used. So, with some trepidation, I made an appointment for her to come and share her expertise.

The appointment was terrible. For what seemed like eternity, this woman went from room to room in my home, criticising everything from the size and shape of each room to the amount of light and position of the furniture. Even some of my most precious ornaments didn't escape her callous comments. I was left reeling, as if I'd just been hit around the head with the latest copy of *House and Home*. After the woman was shown the door, my husband Keith couldn't help but voice his frustration – not with the woman, I might add, as he couldn't care less what she thought – but with me. Why I had let her verbally trash our house? This was our home, and despite the changes we want to make, we still love it just the way it is.

It is the same with Jesus: he loves us all just the way we are, despite all the plans for change he may have for us. He wants us to only be concerned with his loving opinion, not that of anyone else, because in heaven no one else's opinion counts except God's. Yes, he has great plans for us; but he loves us as we are right now, mess and all.

Jesus is a skilled craftsman as well as king. He uses only the costliest of materials in his restoration work. There are no cheap flat-pack mass-produced items in his stores – everything has a high price. I don't know if you have ever 'had the builders in'. As yet, we haven't carried out the major renovation work our house probably needs, but we have had to do some repairs. On one occasion, we discovered a leak which came from under our solid concrete kitchen floor. We called a plumber and the usual scenario ensued: he walked into our kitchen, bent down to take a quick look, stood up with hands on his hips shaking his head and inhaling with a long whistle. This, if you haven't already guessed, means it is going to cost – and cost a lot!

The wonderful thing, though, about the restoration of our individual life house is that Jesus has already paid the price. Everything that Jesus needed to do was done and paid for on the cross. The song 'Here I am to worship' sums it up: "I'll never know how much it cost / To take my sin upon that cross".[6]

So Jesus is not like any earthly builder. He won't look you up and down, shaking his head in bewilderment as to where to start on such an enormous task. No, Jesus rolls up his sleeves, flexes his strong right arm and says with a smile, "Right, I've covered all the costs, let's get to work!" In fact, the price Jesus paid for your sin also included the sin you have yet to commit; it includes both past and future, all paid in full, so you can be free.

Opening up

I once heard it said that "there is nothing as miserable as a born-again sinner" – someone who has accepted Jesus, but nothing in their life has changed. This is what happens if we welcome Jesus in through the front door – and then tell him he can't go in any of the other rooms. It's saying to him, "This far but no further". How sad to keep those doors shut to Jesus. If we've already accepted that we can't hide anything from God, why do we resist his love and offer of free help? He wants to inhabit every room in your life and start a clean-up operation. He wants you to grant him free access to every nook and cranny, every dark and dusty corner. Yes, that will take further steps of faith by trusting Jesus, and yes it may take some time; but you will never be on your own in the process.

In my own life, for many years, I struggled with low self-esteem. By nature, I am quite an extrovert and enjoy company – but deep inside I always felt

---

[6] Tim Hughes (2001) 'Here I am to worship', Worship Together Records

'less' somehow: not that pretty, not that interesting, just not that special at all. In my first book, *Gorgeous: Seeing yourself through God's eyes*,[7] I wrote about my journey of discovering how God really sees me. It was as if there were a full-length mirror in the hallway of my life house – but for so many years all I saw in it was a poor reflection of who I really am. I saw what was behind me – my past, my mistakes, my failures – or just the image I was used to seeing, the self I didn't really like. It took some time, but eventually I decided to accept Jesus' help and his invitation to step 'through the looking glass'. I began to see beyond what my past told me, or what I could see with my own eyes. I learnt that when we look at ourselves in a mirror, what we see and believe of ourselves is often a back-to-front image of who we really are. But God sees the real me: who I was originally meant to be. This journey of seeing and accepting myself the way God sees me continues to this day. And Jesus started to work in me right there in the hallway, before I was even willing to open up a single room!

The transformation begins

Jesus has already planned for you to have the perfect project manager for your restoration – the Holy Spirit. Jesus is the ultimate property developer, but he never sells his property; he lives in it himself, by his Spirit. He loves each one of us so much that he will never leave us nor forsake us. Before his death, Jesus comforted his disciples with a promise that 'the Counsellor', the Holy Spirit, the Spirit of truth, would be with them forever, and would teach them and remind them of everything Jesus had said (see John 14 and 15). The Holy Spirit comes to live within us when we let Jesus into our life house, and this indwelling Spirit is the one who powers the process of change within us.

For a few people, the process of transformation is visible immediately. In her book *Chasing the Dragon*,[8] Jackie Pullinger describes the 'supernatural detox' that

---

[7] Mandy Muckett (2014) *Gorgeous: Seeing yourself through God's eyes*, Evangelista Media
[8] Jackie Pullinger and Andrew Quicke (1980) *Chasing the Dragon*, Hodder & Stoughton

freed heroin addicts in Hong Kong from both physical and spiritual bondage in a very short space of time. But for most of us, myself included, the process is a gradual one. At times it can seem so slow that you feel you're never going to change. But for all of us, whether the process is fast or slow, it lasts a lifetime, completed only when we see Jesus 'face to face'. So, if you are feeling frustrated that you're seeing little progress, I want to encourage you with these words:

> Now the Lord is the Spirit, and where the Spirit of the Lord is, *there is liberty* [emancipation from bondage, true freedom]. And we all, with unveiled face, *continually* seeing as in a mirror the glory of the Lord, are *progressively* being transformed into His image from [one degree of] glory to [even more] glory, which comes from the Lord, [who is] the Spirit'
>
> 2 Corinthians 3:17–18 (AMP)

If the Holy Spirit is the 'power' that enables change, what does this look like in reality? From the outside, it doesn't look like a lot. For all believers, the process begins on the inside, where no one but God can see his own workmanship. At times, we may feel that all we have as evidence of our transformation is our verbal profession of faith in Jesus, trusting that God is in fact at work somewhere in our lives. From the outside, to someone who doesn't have faith, the suggestion of trust in Jesus looks no better than scaffolding – rigid rules of conduct attempting to shore up a crumbling wreck of a building. What they don't see is that for those who believe, the work is taking place inside, underneath the decaying exterior. Over time, no matter how fast (or, more usually, slow) the process, the work that Jesus does on the inside of us begins to shine through so that others will notice a change in us. The restoration of our lives is evidenced as we grow in peace, love, joy and forgiveness.

The next question is: if the Holy Spirit powers my change, do I have any part to play, or is it an automatic process? The incredible thing is – even though Jesus has the perfect plans for our restoration, and has appointed a holy project manager to oversee and guide the work – he invites *us* to partner with him in this awesome 'makeover'.

But what if I don't like what he has planned – what about what *I* want? Will he force his ideas on me without even consulting me? What if I think 'my way' is better? And there you have it, right there: the door we most often refuse to unlock is that of our own free will. I think this quote from Herman Melville's *Moby Dick* sums up our dilemma perfectly: "And if we obey God, we must disobey ourselves; and it is in this disobeying ourselves, wherein the hardness of obeying God consists."[9] Willing *surrender, submission and obedience*: most of us would not find those three words very appealing; scary for some, awful for others. But we often miss the word that precedes them, the word 'willing'. God does not manipulate us to do what he wants. He comes alongside us and works *with* us so that we are joyful and fulfilled in giving ourselves wholly and completely to his ways, his plans, and ultimately his will for us.

The strength of the human will is amazing. It was created to be that way, with full freedom of choice; but since that original eviction from our first garden home, our will has been increasingly influenced by a deceiving voice. Jesus called the devil a liar and "the father of lies", and our enemy Satan will say anything that will keep us from agreement with God, especially when it comes to the plans God has for our lives. You can get no better clarification than Jesus' own words: "the thief comes only in order to steal and kill and destroy. I came that they may have *and* enjoy life, and have it in abundance (to the full, till it overflows)" (John 10:10 AMP). A deceived will believes that transformation can be achieved solely through personal effort. I repeat: the devil is a liar and he is incapable of creating or restoring anything. He only offers a counterfeit resemblance of restoration as he whispers to our will, urging us to accept his version of an inferior design.

Like a demonic estate agent he tries to sell us the idea of transformation by self-effort alone, embellishing half-truths to tempt us into the believing the lie that we don't need God's help.[10] Cleaning up your life house through your

---

[9] Melville, H., Parker, H. and Hayford, H. (2002) *Moby-Dick (6th edition)*, Norton
[10] Apologies to any estate agents reading this metaphor! I'm sure you are lovely and God loves you just as much as he does me, and please forgive my attempt at humour

own strength may impress others that you are a 'good person', but God can see through your facade. It's useless to strive for transformation by the will alone, without acknowledging Jesus' death on the cross to free us, or the power of the Holy Spirit to change us. And it opens us up to the slavery of (empty) religious efforts. Jesus had much say to the people in his time who faked righteousness. Interestingly, it was the Pharisees and teachers of religious law that he reserved his deepest contempt for:

> "You're hopeless, you religion scholars and Pharisees! Frauds! You're like manicured grave plots, grass clipped and the flowers bright, but six feet down its all rotting bones and worm-eaten flesh. People look at you and think you're saints, but beneath the skin you're total frauds."
>
> Matthew 23:27–28 (MSG)

All fake transformation is called 'works of the flesh'. What does this mean? All humans are triune beings, made up of a physical body, a soul and a spirit.[11] When we try to change ourselves using our own strength we lead with our 'flesh', or old fallen nature. This means that our physical body with its natural demands leads the way, followed by our soul (mind, will and emotions) in self-centred agreement with the body, with our pitiful human spirit trailing far behind – but this is not the order God intended.

God created us as spiritual beings: we are souls, housed in physical bodies. And we have spirits, the vital part of us that relates to God, designed to draw life from him. It is only when we operate in God's intended order – our spirits leading and drawing strength from God, followed by our souls, then our bodies – that we can achieve lasting, visible change. Our spirit needs to work in agreement with the Holy Spirit, because he alone has the power to restore us. "Not by might or by power but by my Spirit says the Lord Almighty" (Zech 4:6b).

---

[11] The teaching of my South African friend, Amanda Buys, is a great resource for an in-depth understanding of our triune nature, and I can highly recommend her series *Journey 2 Freedom*. See https://www.kanaanministries.org/downloads/

So, are you ready to change? There are many words used in the Bible to describe how we agree with God's lordship of our lives. As I've just mentioned, words like 'obey' and 'submit' aren't very attractive to us. But how about looking at it another way? Letting Jesus be Lord simply means giving a 'Yes' to him, allowing his Spirit to take the lead in every decision, in every area of our lives. If you want to do this, all you have to do is welcome the Holy Spirit and hand over the 'keys' of your will, allowing him free access to all the rooms of your life house.

Ready? You can say it after me…

"Yes Lord! Come Holy Spirit!"

RESTORATION REFLECTIONS

Choose one of the scenes below, then close your eyes and ask God to guide your imagination as you picture it. You might find it helpful to write down or draw what you saw in your mind's eye afterwards.

- You go to visit God the carpenter, who made you. You enter his workshop and he sees you, turning and picking you up carefully with his huge calloused but gentle hands. He looks pleased that you have come to him. Ask him any question you like, such as 'Why did you decide to create me?' 'How do you feel about me?'

How does he answer you?

- Jesus has walked through the front door and is standing in the hallway of your home. How do you respond? Do you stand and stare – or kneel – or fall prostrate? Look at his face. Can you see love, acceptance and compassion? What does he say to you?

TALK TO THE ARCHITECT

Jesus, I ask you today to begin your work in my life. Please show me the plans you have for my restoration and where you want to start.

Come, Holy Spirit! I say 'Yes' to you. I hand over to you, as my holy project manager, the keys to the rooms in my life house and give you permission to open up any locked doors so that Jesus can change me from the inside out. Amen.

CHAPTER 4
BUILT ON THE ROCK

Do you remember the three little pigs? The first little pig builds a house out of straw and the second out of sticks, both building quickly to put in the least possible effort. The third little pig, however, takes more time and builds his house out of bricks. As the story goes, the big bad wolf comes after the little pigs. He comes 'huffing and puffing', rampaging straight through the first two flimsily built houses, with the owners having to seek shelter with their wiser sibling in his sturdy brick house.

How are you building?

Why do I remind you of this childhood story? Well, it leads me to ask you: how are you building your life house? The story of the little pigs describes how they built the walls and roofs of their houses. What about your walls and roof? Does your wealth and reputation make up a large part of the walls of your life? Do you feel secure because of the large number of friends you believe you have? Does your level of health help you appear stronger than others around you? Perhaps your stability and security come from the country you live in or the perceived strength of its economy, government or military capability? Whatever it is, just like the little pigs, there is one fundamental omission: there is no mention of *foundations* for any of their houses.

Now of course, you could skip the foundations and start building a house with its walls resting directly on the dirt – but you should first consider the famous Bible story about house-building wisdom, the story of the wise and foolish builders (Matt 7:24–27). One man built his house on the sand; a storm came and his house was destroyed. The other wisely built his house on the rock, and when a storm came it did not fall. It is exactly the same with building our own lives. What foundation is your life built on? And what would happen to it if you had to face a storm? Our world is in a constant state of change. What once was firm and secure may feel unstable and can even unexpectedly sweep you off your feet.

Unlike my husband, I love watching those TV programmes of short video clips of people in real-life funny – or perhaps not so funny – situations. My absolute number one favourite clip is of a poor woman in a 'fun house' at the fair. It's one of those amusement rides where you walk through a collection of crazy rooms with uneven floor and moving walls, disorienting your mind and tricking your body. In this clip, the unsuspecting woman is trying to navigate her way along a moving walkway. Not too difficult you may think – they have those at airports, don't they? Not this kind they don't. Before she knows it, the walkway that was smoothly travelling in one direction abruptly switches and starts moving in the opposite direction. The woman tries to correct her balance but before she can, the walkway has resumed its previous direction. Back and forth, back and forth the walkway moves, ending with her sitting unceremoniously on her bottom, unable even to stand.

This clip still makes me laugh after the umpteenth time – but what if that silly situation were your daily experience? What if you were a yo-yo dieter or excessive spender, losing weight only to put on more than you lost, or trying to clear your credit card debt only to max it out again the following month? What if the certainties of your life suddenly become so unstable that you felt like the proverbial rug had been pulled from under your feet – perhaps by losing your job or going through a divorce? That would not be funny at all. But there is one thing we can depend on. The Bible tells us of a God who is dependable, never changing and always there for us:

> In the beginning, you laid the foundations of the earth,
> and the heavens are the work of your hands.
> They will perish, but you remain;
> they will all wear out like a garment.

> Like clothing you will change them
> and they will be discarded.
> But you remain the same,
> and your years will never end.
>
> Psalm 102: 25–27

Yes, the Bible emphatically states that, "Jesus Christ is the same yesterday and today and forever" (Heb 13:8). Building our house on rock means building our lives on Jesus' teaching and unfailing love, and when the storms come, we will not fall. Jesus used the imagery of building on rock, not only for our individual lives, but in speaking to Peter about the church: "And I tell you that you are Peter, and on this rock I will build my church, and the gates of Hades will not overcome it" (Matt 16:18). Anything built on the rock of faith in Jesus is so strong that even all the powers of hell ('Hades') cannot destroy its foundation. There is an absolute assurance in God's message to us. It remains steadfast and true. Nothing can shake God. When we invite Jesus into our life house, he himself is the firm foundation on which our renovations can begin. His love and purposes for us are secured: "For he chose us in him before the creation of the world to be holy and blameless in his sight. In love he predestined us for adoption to sonship through Jesus Christ, in accordance with his pleasure and will" (Eph 1:4–5).

And as if that wasn't enough, the verse continues (in the Message version):

> It's in Christ that we find out who we are and what we are living for. Long before we first heard of Christ and got our hopes up, he had his eye on us, had designs on us for glorious living, part of the overall purpose he is working out in everything and everyone.
> It's in Christ that you, once you heard the truth and believed it (this Message of your salvation), found yourselves home free—signed, sealed, and delivered by the Holy Spirit. This signet from God is the first instalment on what's coming, a reminder that we'll get everything God has planned for us, a praising and glorious life.
>
> Ephesians 1: 11–14 (MSG)

You might still be clinging to the idea of DIY. You may have tried in vain to underpin your own sagging foundations, only for them to fail again when any pressure was exerted. But Jesus will not allow shoddy work; for him there are no shortcuts. He will build using his foundation of love alone. In fact, Jesus *is* the cornerstone of this firm foundation (a name given to him in Ephesians 2:20). In an architectural sense, the cornerstone or foundation stone is the first stone set in place when the foundation is built; it is vitally important as it provides a reference for all the other stones that are laid. This cornerstone determines the whole structure. When Jesus is our cornerstone, the other parts of our life can fall into place.

Troubles – and glory

Returning to the story of the little pigs, that big bad wolf (who we might cast as the devil in our own life stories) destroyed the houses made with weak materials – those that could not withstand the attack. I find it interesting that all the wolf did was blow on the houses. It's as if the devil only needs to speak out words over our lives to demolish them. As I said before, the devil is a liar. He delights in whispering half truths about our identies and destinies. He tells us we are alone in our troubles when we are not: God never leaves or forsakes us. He tries to convince us that we have no value and are of no consequence: but God considers us so precious he sent his only son into the world to die in our place. We will all experience troubles in our lives – we will feel the huff and puff of the wolf's breath – but our foundations are secure.

And in the midst of those troubles we must remember, "…in all things God works for the good of those who love him, who have been called according to his purpose" (Rom 8:28). Whether our problems are illness, unemployment, loss or persecution – to name but a few – "…our light and momentary troubles are achieving for us an eternal glory that far outweighs them all" (2 Cor 4:17). How do our troubles achieve glory? Well, I think it has something to do with us becoming a reflection of Jesus and his glory; our lives being built not with perishable material like straw and sticks, but spiritually rebuilt on the imperishable love of God. His love is stronger than brick; people who have experienced hurricanes, earthquakes or tsunamis can tell you that even bricks can become like Lego blocks when up against the worst natural forces.

Our God is such a wonderful creator that he only uses the most precious of materials to renovate your life. Just consider if he wanted to rebuild using pure gold as his chosen medium: your life would be as precious as gold, shining out his glory for all who meet you. Can you even begin to imagine that? But did you know how gold is treated to make it as durable as it can be? It's heated to high temperatures in a process called tempering. God uses this same process in our renovation, but his tempering comes in the form of testing.

Children go to school, are taught facts and then tested by being asked to recall what they've already learnt. God's classroom is somewhat different. We are given a test to sit without having learnt the subject, required to depend solely on our teacher, the Holy Spirit. We are tested in our level of belief and trust in God. It is then only in hindsight that our learning comes – after the test. It is indeed a back-to-front, upside-down kingdom principal.

Much of my own process of renovation has come during times of difficulty or suffering, as my life is tested and tempered by the Lord; as a result, his purposes for my life now shine out for all to see. Our lives have an eternal relevance, expressed not in our temporal circumstances but by *our response to God through them.* If you have regretted the waste of years before you allowed Jesus to begin his work on your life house, don't despair. Be comforted by this: 'I am convinced *and* confident of this very thing, that he who has begun a good work in you will [continue to] perfect *and* complete it until the day of Christ Jesus [the time of His return]' (Phil 1:6 AMP). And it's in those times of trouble that he may, unperceived by you, be getting the most renovation work done.

The little mud hut built on the rock

What does it look like, in real life, when someone's life is built on Jesus' foundations? I'll finish this chapter by sharing an example with you.

Keith and I are passionate advocates of the Christian child sponsorship charity Compassion International.[12] We sponsor four children through their programme, and regularly volunteer to tell people about the awesome work the charity does in releasing children from poverty.

One of our sponsored children is called Shadrack, and he lives in Kenya. Recently we had the wonderful opportunity to go on an 'insight trip' to see the work Compassion does, and as part of this trip we got to meet Shadrack face to face for the very first time. We have been sponsoring him for many years and had longed to finally meet him. The experience was extremely emotional, and certainly a highlight of our trip; but I had another experience in Kenya that has changed me forever.

Our group were taken to see the work of a project based in the Maasai Mara tribal area. In the morning, we spent our time with the children who attend the project, seeing the activities they enjoyed – writing letters to their sponsors, learning new skills and crafts, and simply being kids and playing. In the afternoon, we had the great privilege of visiting a sponsored child named John and his mother Mary in their home.

A home it certainly was, but to our Western eyes it was the tiniest hut made of mud. Now, I'm a woman of ample proportions, and I became quite concerned that I couldn't even fit through the tiny opening that acted as the door. The local pastor entered first and reached out for my hand to guide me in – and a guide is what I needed, for although I got through the door, it was absolutely pitch black inside this little hut. Once my eyes adjusted to what light there was, I discovered that we stood in a two-roomed space lit only by a candle stub.

The first thing that struck me though was not how small the home was, but how very neat and tidy. Everything had its place, from the line of mugs that sat side by side, to the orderliness of the bed pallet that doubled as our makeshift seat. We spent some time with Mary and her son. He proudly showed us all the letters his American sponsor had sent him. This precious bundle was securely stored in a battered tin box.

Nearing the end of our visit, I was asked to pray and bless the family before

---

[12] See the Compassion International child sponsorship programme at https://www.compassion.com/, www.compassionuk.org and https://compassion.ch/

we left. I asked Mary what she wanted prayer for. She said she was asking God – and trusting in him – that he would provide enough so that all her children could go to school. I was struck by this simple yet powerful request, and her full assurance that God would provide; she knew she could ask God for her needs to be met without fear or doubt. She just asked, based on her firm faith in Jesus. We finished our visit, having prayed for and blessed Mary and her family with some practical food stuffs as thanks for her time.

We made our way back into the dazzling light of the African sun, and as we said our final goodbyes and thanks, Mary produced gifts she had made for us. With great humility, she offered us each a handmade necklace, placing it gently over our heads. When my turn came to receive my gift I burst into tears. You see, my mind could not comprehend what was happening. Here we were, a small group of Western travellers who obviously have so much more materially than Mary could ever dream of. Yet it was Mary who gave *us* gifts! With such generosity of spirit, she wanted to bless us! To put it simply, I was undone.

I think Mary was a little bemused by my reaction – she just smiled and gave a little laugh and nod of recognition, one sister in Christ to another. One sister who absolutely knew the assurance of Jesus in her life, despite her worldly lack – to me, who was only just learning how to live freely in that same loving assurance.

So, as I dry my eyes and stop my snivels, let us look to our saviour Jesus. He has moved on and now really wants to get our home transformed. Onwards and upwards my friend! I think that's him, can you see him? He's up on the roof.

RESTORATION REFLECTION

Choose one of the scenes below, then close your eyes and ask God to guide your imagination as you picture it. You might find it helpful to write down or draw what you saw in your mind's eye afterwards.

- You are standing with Jesus in the hallway of your home. When you are ready, say to Jesus, "Show me what my life is built on." The building around you now vanishes, leaving you standing in the exposed foundations. What are those foundations made of? Are they strong?

- You are at a fun fair, on a walkway that keeps changing direction. The walkway could represent difficult circumstances in your life, either now or in the past. It's very hard to stay on your feet, but you can't get off until the ride is over. Jesus is next to you and wants to help. What does he say to you?

TALK TO THE ARCHITECT

Lord Jesus, please forgive me where I've tried to build my life based on the wrong foundations. I ask you to come and be my immoveable cornerstone.

Holy Spirit, I give you permission to dig as deep into my life as you need, to remove anything that is unstable. I trust your foundations – even when the storms come, I shall not be moved. Amen.

CHAPTER 5
UP ON THE ROOF

Ask any builder and they will tell you that it's pointless remodelling a home unless you have two essential matters seen to. The first is the foundations, as we've just seen; and now Jesus wants to turn your attention to the next vital issue – the roof. Is it weatherproof? There's no point carefully restoring your home and filling it with wonderful furnishings if it's practically open to the elements. A builder will want to make a home watertight as soon as possible.

Sealing your roof

When you give over your life to Jesus, a mysterious event happens; something that can't be seen but happens nonetheless. When the Holy Spirit comes into our lives we become 'sealed': "it is he who has also put his seal on us [that is, he has appropriated us and certified us as his] and has given us the [Holy] Spirit in our hearts as a pledge [like a security deposit to guarantee the fulfilment of his promise of eternal life]" (2 Cor 1:22 AMP). We become carriers of the Holy Spirit. We become part of God's family forever, and this places us under the authority and protection of Christ himself. His Spirit in us confirms and guarantees his protection, like the wax seal on an ancient legal document. It is the same with the roof on your home: it serves as a covering, a protection.

The Bible has much to say about how God protects and covers his people. In the Passover story, the Israelites were told to paint the blood of a lamb over their front doors to protect them from the angel of death as he 'passed over' to carry out judgment on the Egyptians (Ex 12). It's as if the roof of our life house – if we have put our trust in Jesus the lamb of God – were covered by a crimson cloak of his blood. The psalms especially tell of God's protection over us: "But let all who take refuge *and* put their trust in You rejoice, let them ever sing for joy; Because You cover *and* shelter them" (Ps 5:1 AMP). God is called our refuge, in other words, our safe place (Ps 46:1 and 57:1). The imagery of a high tower or fortress is also often used to portray just how protected we are by God. Psalm 91 uses a different image, that of a mother hen covering her chicks with her wings. I recommend you take a look at this beautiful psalm if you've never read it before – perhaps even bookmark or highlight it to read in times of trouble or distress.

But being protected by God doesn't necessarily mean that as Christians we won't experience harm. If any religious leader tells you different, don't believe them. No, believers will experience pain, loss, illness and death just like everyone else. In fact, Christians are being persecuted and killed in greater numbers throughout the world in this century than ever before. So, what do I mean by 'protection'? Now, just to be clear, I do believe in God's ability to heal supernaturally and to protect miraculously. But what I want to talk about here is spiritual protection: God guarding us in a realm that is beyond the physical, body and soul.

You may be wondering why we need spiritual protection. Isn't physical protection enough to makes us feel secure? These days, the need to feel secure is uppermost in many people's minds – the world we live in is not necessarily a safe place. How then, have you tried to protect yourself? Are you like me, a person who has tried to control everything and everyone around them in order to feel safe? Or are you one of those more laid back folk who, for an easy life, will just comply – go with the flow – to not make waves? Perhaps your sense of safety comes from being like the proverbial ostrich who sticks his head in the sand and foolishly believes that if I can't see danger then it can't be happening? Or are you one of life's brawlers, who comes out fighting and whose perceived safety is sought by hitting first and asking questions later? Whatever our chosen method of self-protection, none of these ways will work for us spiritually.

I once heard it said that Christians are 'born on a battlefield' – the spiritual battle that rages around us and often within us. The Bible is full of stories of battles won and lost, but I want to remind you that the greatest battle of all time – and the one which ensures your protection like a strong, sturdy roof – was the battle Jesus won for you on the cross. Jesus himself said, "It is finished" (John 19:30). The war was won at Calvary that day over two thousand years ago. But at the same time, the fight goes on.

At the end of the Second World War, when the allies' enemy was officially defeated, it took some time for all the fighting to come to an end. Some factions hadn't heard – or wouldn't accept – the news of their defeat. Spiritually, we live in a similar age. Although heaven's war is won, God has not yet brought his kingdom fully to earth or shut down the actions of the enemy. We still need to stand. So "our struggle is not against flesh and blood, but against the rulers, against the powers of this dark world and against the spiritual forces of evil in the heavenly realms" (Eph 6:12). Forgive me for using a Star Trek analogy – but as chief engineer Scotty might have said, "We've got Klingons off our starboard bow Captain!"[13]

Jesus wants to protect you. He will ensure that your roof of self-reliance is lovingly dismantled; he knows it isn't strong enough to withstand the spiritual storms that the enemy will send your way. But have no fear – God supplies his protection in the Spirit by covering us, or putting it another way, 'hiding' us in Christ himself (Col 3:3). And that, my friends, is a whole universe better than the protection even the most famous star ship captain can offer.

Being spiritually protected means we can have joy even in the most distressing times. It enables us to have peace when chaos is all around. His protection brings hope in the most hopeless of situations and strengthens us when we are at our weakest.

---

[13] The Star Trek TV series was created by Gene Roddenberry and first shown on 8 September 1966. See www.startrek.com

When you are weak, he is strong

God's strength, and how he uses it for our protection, is one of his greatest and most misunderstood qualities.

We often understand God's strength as a powerful force that comes from a vengeful, violent God. We might compare our heavenly father to some type of Zeus character from Greek mythology – all retribution and thunderbolts, a god who can squash our enemies like an elephant stomping on an ant. But the Bible tells us that it's in *weakness* that God's strength is found. It was in the context of weakness that the Holy Spirit once spoke to me about Jesus' protection.

One Sunday morning I was listening to one of our pastors, Silvia Nickelson, preach on Jesus's words to the apostle Paul:

> "But he said to me, 'My grace is sufficient for you, for my power is made perfect in weakness.' Therefore, I will boast all the more gladly about my weakness, so that Christ's power may rest on me. That is why, for Christ's sake, I delight in weakness, in insults, in hardships, persecutions, in difficulties. For when I am weak, then I am strong."
>
> 2 Corinthians 12: 9–12

As Silvia spoke, I sensed the Holy Spirit say that even at our weakest, even if we can do nothing else, all we need do is *say the name of Jesus*. I reflected on this, and a question popped into my mind. I asked the Holy Spirit, "Why do demons flee at the name of Jesus?" I was stunned when I heard the reply. He said:

> Demons flee at the name of Jesus because:
> His presence panics them
> His goodness grieves them.
> His wisdom wounds them.
> His mercy mystifies them.
> His love lacerates them.
> His righteousness repulses them.

His humility hammers them.
His peace pierces them like a million nails.
His truth tortures them.
His compassion cuts them.
His holiness hurts them.
His beauty blinds them.
His word silences them.
His meekness maddens them.
His counsel confuses them.
His grace guillotines them
AND
His blood binds and burns them for eternity.

So for Jesus, some of the most deadly weapons in his spiritual armoury are peace, compassion and meekness! These are certainly not the world's weapons. And when we are feeling weak and desperate, we don't have to muster our own peace, compassion and so on – we can simply call on his name and he supplies it all.

Admitting that we need protection proclaims, "I am weak!" and none of us really wants to broadcast that to the world. Being weak is hardly considered a positive quality. Yet God wants us to live completely free in a loving relationship that is *dependent* upon him. And that's what makes us strong.

Our high places

Jesus has detailed plans to renovate our roofs. As he replaces our old, broken self-reliance with his strong covering of protection, he also wants to clear out our dark, cobweb-filled attic space of anything that will elevate itself above him.

The Israelites were given this commandment: "You shall have no other gods before me" (Ex 20:3), and when they entered the promised land, "Destroy completely all the places on the high mountains, on the hills and under every spreading tree, where the nations you are dispossessing worship their gods" (Deut 12:2). Sadly, God's people chose instead to use these 'high places' for their own form of worship, often to other gods. As followers of Christ we can make the same mistake. What cherished things do we keep in our own 'high places'?

One of the things we can elevate is ourselves. It was in my case. Here's how Jesus began to restore the attic of my own 'life house'. (As I said earlier, we are on a journey together and I don't want you to feel you're the only one who needs Jesus to transform their life!) This happened early on in my walk with Jesus, through my practice of journaling personal prayers. As I described in Chapter 2, while praying I saw a picture in my mind of an old-fashioned fairground that I was walking around with Jesus. Each ride represented a specific sin in my life. Jesus showed me his perspective on my life, and this experience has been an important part of my own renovation process. This is what I wrote in my journal.

The helter-skelter of pride

So here I am again Lord. Please forgive my futile attempts at running from your arms, your offer of healing and abundant life.

We are in the fairground again and we walk on, Jesus and I, to the next ride. I'm reminded of Old England: nostalgia for my childhood, memories of country fairs and bygone times, when everything seemed so much simpler, and summer meant sunshine, ice cream cones and candy floss.

A grand red-and-white striped helter-skelter stands before us. It is a regal tower, with a spiral staircase and slide, just waiting to be climbed. It's so high! I want to be up there above everyone else, looking down on them all like ants. I look to Jesus. He nods his head – not in agreement of my desires, but in his sovereign acknowledgement of my choice. As I grab my mat and start to climb the wooden stairs inside the tower I hear Jesus speaking ... "I am the Alpha and the Omega, says the Lord God, who is and who was and who is to come, the Almighty" (Revn 1:8). "Yes, yes, I know", I think to myself flippantly. I know he's the sovereign Lord, but I'm less interested in him and more interested in getting to the top.

I take step after step, but very quickly I remember that I hate climbing stairs! All that never-ending drudge and effort. I pull on the hand rail to take the strain from my burning knees. My arms are feeble and my knees weak but my will drives me on, higher and higher. I push past slower people. I deserve to be first to the top! The stairs are steeper now and my breath is laboured. A gargantuan effort is required to get up the last few steps, my will battling my aching body. I will be the best, I will excel and be excellent, acknowledged by all.

I've made it! I punch the air in triumph, full of pride. The top of the helter-skelter is open to the sky and I can see the whole fair sprawled below me. I feel so important up here, and for a second I enjoy the position of power. Jesus, too, was taken to a high point like this and offered all the kingdoms of the world and their splendour if he would but bow down and worship Satan. Right now I feel the same – the difference being that he was tempted, but didn't sin.

I spot Jesus below me – he is shouting something I pretend I can't quite hear, but I know what it is: "Pride goes before destruction, a haughty spirit before a fall" (Prov 16:18). I turn away so I can't see him, but I'm too late to stop the inevitable. Others have reached the top too now and they want their own moment of glory. There is only room for one up here and it's my turn to get pushed. The mat I was holding is wrenched from my hand and thrown down the black chute that gapes before me like the mouth of a giant man-eating snake. I fall head first down the slide, tumbling head over heels. I grab frantically at anything that might slow my descent.

In an instant I am unceremoniously spewed out at the bottom of the slide, landing face first in the mud. I lift my head out of the mire and the first thing I see are Jesus' feet. I hear him laughing! He's not ridiculing me though; his laugh is full of compassion and mercy. The Spirit of God reminds me, "Therefore God exalted him to the highest place and gave him the name that is above every name, that at the name of Jesus every knee should bow, in heaven and on the earth and under the earth and every tongue confess that Jesus Christ is Lord, to the glory of God the Father" (Phi 2:9–11). My climb of pride only landed me in the mud – whereas Jesus's sacrifice has given him the highest place forever.

Jesus helps me to my feet and wipes the mud from my cheeks. I blush at his kindness, and my own arrogance.

"When will I get over myself, Jesus?" I ask.

He winks at me, as if to say that everything will be okay in the end. I'm in awe, all over again, that the king of the universe is so intimate with me.

"I love you, Lord," I blurt.
"I know you do, Mandy," he smiles, as we walk on.

Yes, my friend – this is the sin of pride. We use it to protect ourselves, to feel secure and high above others. Pride can present an immaculate and impressive façade, but in truth is like a roof with broken and missing tiles. Instead of protecting us it does the complete opposite. It not only leaves us unprotected but leads us to fall, laying bare our brokenness beneath. Our pride is a sin that Jesus wants to remove; because the highest place in our hearts is to be reserved for the only one worthy of it, Jesus Christ himself. You may not experience a picture in your mind exactly as I did, but Jesus will have his own plans to topple pride from its high place in your life house. When we ask Jesus, he shows us what our pride looks like and what he wants to do about it. Some of us won't even need to ask, because we know without being told. Whatever it looks like and however it is revealed, we have no need to fear.

Let's draw closer to Jesus, listen to his plan of works for our new roof, and by our confession allow him to start this crucial part of the renovation process. (And if we get close enough, we might even get a wink.)

RESTORATION REFLECTIONS

Choose one of the scenes below, then close your eyes and ask God to guide your imagination as you picture it. You might find it helpful to write down or draw what you saw in your mind's eye afterwards.

- You are standing with Jesus up on the roof of your home. Ask him, "Show me how I protect myself." What do you see when you look at the roof, your protection – what's it made of? Is it blood-red, reflecting Jesus' work on the cross? Or is it made of something else? And is it doing a good job of protecting you, or is it broken and leaking?

- You are standing with Jesus at the bottom of a ladder that leads up to your attic. You know that the attic holds the things you value above all others. Ask Jesus, "Show me what I keep up there." Then follow Jesus up the ladder into the loft. What, or who, do you see?

TALK TO THE ARCHITECT

Lord Jesus, thank you that I am protected by the blood you shed and the victory you won for me on the cross, because I believe in you. If I have relied on anything other than you to protect me, please forgive me, and help me dismantle it.

Holy Spirit, thank you that my life is forever sealed in you! I can have joy, peace and hope, no matter what comes against me.

Heavenly Father, I am weak but you have given me all the strength I need in the name of your son, Jesus. Your strength is made perfect in my weakness. Thank you Father. Amen.

CHAPTER 6
THE HEART OF THE HOME

It is said that that the kitchen is the heart of any home; so the kitchen, my friend, is the first actual room that we will enter in our 'life house', and in this room we can begin to explore together the mystery of the human heart.

Traditionally, we see the heart as the place where love is birthed and nurtured. In a physical sense our hearts are the power houses of our bodies: ever beating, always in action, pumping life blood around our bodies. In the same way, the kitchen of our life house needs to pump love into every other part. Love is more than just an emotion, more than the firing of specific neurones in the brain or surges of hormones. No, in its purest form, love is spiritual; the very essence of life itself.

Learning to love

Just as no one is born knowing how to cook, but we learn it as a crucial life skill, so we must learn the most important life skill of all – to receive love, and give it in return. First and foremost, you learn that you are loved. In doing so you learn to love yourself; this then enables you to love others. These three steps are the ABC of life school.

So, do you love yourself? Not in a selfie, narcissistic, Instagram way, but really love and value who you are, as you are, right now? Not a future you, the 'only when' kind – only when you've lost that weight or you've got that job, or you've met 'the one'. Maybe loving yourself is something you have yet to learn. Did you ever experience licking the spoon after watching (or even helping) your mother or grandmother as she made cookies or cakes in the kitchen? That was the start of learning to cook. Learning to love yourself is the same process – you need to have it demonstrated to you first, in order that you know how to love. Because before you can even love God, you need to experience his love for you.

No matter how little love you experienced as a child, you can know God's love for you. God loves everyone – he cannot do anything else but love, as he *is* love (1 John 4:8). If you have invited Jesus to live with you in your life house, you can truly start learning about love in its purest form. While people who haven't invited Jesus into their lives yet can of course experience love for themselves and for others to a certain degree, why not go straight to the source of love itself, and ask him to live in you? There is a huge difference.

The four loves

The Bible describes more than one type of love. In the Greek used in the New Testament, there are three main words for human love:

- *Storge*: familial love like that between parent and child.
- *Eros*: sexual love. This is where we get the word 'erotic'. It involves our physical bodies and is a self-centred love.
- *Phileo*: affectionate love, such as for friends. This involves our soul, mind and emotions.

But history shows time and again that human attempts to love always become a kind of futile tug-of-war: between our own selfish desires on one side, and our guilt at not being able to love enough on the other. We can be so self-centered that we only experience or offer a shallow, counterfeit love, which cannot sustain anyone.

However, there is a fourth love. In this chapter I want to concentrate on this type: *agape*. It is the love that only God can supply; a supernatural love. It is divine and 'other-centered' in its nature. It is sacrificial, a poured-out kind of love; having received this divine love in its purest form, you cannot help yourself but give it away to someone else. This perfect form of love is not only more than sufficient to sustain us, but grows stronger the more we freely give it away. It is true that "we love because he [God] first loved us" (1 John 4:19). Learning to first receive God's *agape* love is essential in the process of learning to love yourself.

Agape is wonderfully described in this well-known Bible passage:

> Love never gives up.
> Love cares more for others than for self.
> Love doesn't want what it doesn't have.
> Love doesn't strut,
> Doesn't have a swelled head,
> Doesn't force itself on others,
> Isn't always "me first,"
> Doesn't fly off the handle,
> Doesn't keep score of the sins of others,
> Doesn't revel when others grovel,
> Takes pleasure in the flowering of truth,
> Puts up with anything,
> Trusts God always,
> Always looks for the best, never looks back, but keeps going to the end.
> 1 Corinthians 13:4–6 (MSG)

To love is to give

Here I want to pause, and tell you an important lesson I've recently learnt about expressing love to another person.

I am a leader in a women's ministry here in Basel called 'Saphira' (a take on the German word for 'sapphire'). We host regular events throughout the year to encourage women as they walk life's path with Jesus. One event was held just before Christmas and included a gift exchange. We had encouraged our guests to bring along a piece of jewellery, an accessory, or a handbag to swap. The idea was to bring something that, although treasured and possibly with sentimental value, was to be freely and joyously given to another woman.

And as it was Christmas we suggested that the gift be wrapped accordingly, with beautiful paper and ribbons – just as you would wrap a gift for someone you loved dearly.

At the event, the women were invited to the gift table and each chose the package that took their liking. As you can imagine, the woman really enjoyed this part of the evening. Much excitement ensued as each one shook and squeezed her gift, wondering what might be inside. Then there was the surprise of discovering what was hidden within all the shiny paper.

As leaders, our team waited until every woman had chosen her gift before we took our turn. Now to tell you something else about myself, I love presents – the bigger the better! I'm a sucker for an exquisitely wrapped box or package. More is more, in my opinion. So it was some surprise to me that when I came to the table to choose my gift, I found myself hesitating to take the biggest and most beautiful gift that remained. I knew it was one of those Holy Spirit nudges, and as I paused, I quietly asked Jesus what gift he would choose for me. To my shock, he directed my eyes to a little white box. The only decoration was a simple thin white bow. To say the decoration was minimal was an understatement. This box did not stand out in any way, yet I was drawn to it like no other on the table. Against my normal instincts, I picked the box up and returned to my seat.

To be honest with you, I wasn't expecting much. I slipped off the little ribbon and removed the lid. What I first saw was cotton wool. Lifting this away, I discovered what Jesus had chosen for me, and it left me speechless. Under the cotton wool lay an intricate silver necklace set with ruby red garnets. Not only that, but a delicate bracelet of the same design, together with a matching ring! A full set of beautiful jewellery had lain hidden in this simple little box. The women around me gasped, as I sat dumbfounded.

As it turned out, unknown to me, this precious gift was donated by my pastor Silvia Nickelson. She came up to me just after I had opened the little box to express her delight that it was me who picked it. Earlier that evening she had watched as the other women chose their gifts and was disappointed that no one had chosen hers. She went on to tell me that the decision to give the jewellery was not an easy one. She had asked Jesus to show her what she should donate and struggled when he highlighted to her this whole set, as it was a gift she had received on her wedding day. Silvia went on to say that she had checked with Larwin, her husband, and both decided to do what Jesus had asked – and to give what was loved away. As well as selecting the gift, Jesus had directed her to wrap it as simply as she could. After explaining all this she looked at me and asked if it was okay? Did I in fact like the gift? I was under no obligation to wear it if I didn't like it.

Oh, how awful I felt in that moment! Not that I didn't like the gift; it was gorgeous. But the Holy Spirit was reminding me of an opportunity he'd given me to show love, and instead I chose compromise. When deciding what I should give to the gift exchange, Jesus had suggested that I too give something precious: the single strand of pearls given to me by my late grandmother. That was his choice – and I decided against it. I donated quite a few items to the exchange: a beautiful scarf, a couple of pretty bracelets and a classic leather wallet, but none of these things were precious to me. It didn't cost me anything in the giving, it wasn't a 'love offering' – more like a chance to declutter my possessions.

That evening I learnt a hard lesson about expressing love. The next week, over coffee, I told Silvia what had happened and why my response was so muted. She didn't burden me with guilt, but just encouraged me in my struggle. She said that Jesus loved me and intended that I should have those lovely garnets. At our Christmas celebration, I did indeed wear the jewellery which perfectly matched a dress I already had in my wardrobe, although I did feel a little embarrassed when my pastor Larwin told me that the jewels really suited me. However, I was overjoyed to know that Silvia was delighted to receive my grandmother's pearls, which I had decided rightly belonged where Jesus wanted them. They looked beautiful around Silvia's neck that evening as she told me how much she loved pearls. And to end my story, we had such an abundance of gifts that evening, we were able to give them to the church's outreach to refugee women as well. Those who had so few worldly possessions would receive a Christmas gift too, inspired by the love of Jesus.

The problem with our hearts

It is said that you can't give away what you don't have; and this is so true when it comes to love. All of us, to some degree or other, have barriers – or keeping to the house theme, locked doors – when it comes to receiving love, and in turn our ability to show it. There are many reasons why we lock those doors. C. S. Lewis explains this perfectly:

"To love at all is to be vulnerable. Love anything and your heart will be wrung and possibly broken. If you want to make sure of keeping it intact you must give it to no one, not even an animal. Wrap it carefully round with hobbies and little luxuries; avoid all entanglements. Lock it up safe in the casket or coffin of your selfishness. But in that casket, safe, dark, motionless, airless, it will change. It will not be broken; it will become unbreakable, impenetrable, irredeemable. To love is to be vulnerable."[14]

The Bible often speaks of people having 'hard hearts', such as in Isaiah: "Go and tell this people: "Be ever hearing, but never understanding; be ever seeing, but never perceiving. Make the heart of this people calloused; make their ears dull and close their eyes. Otherwise they might see with their eyes, hear with their ears, understand with their hearts, and turn and be healed" (Is 9:6–10). Or this: "The heart is deceitful above all things and it is extremely sick; who can understand it fully *and* know its secret motives?" (Jer 17:9 AMP). Scripture also warns, "Above all else, guard your heart, for everything you do flows from it" (Prov 4:23).

And the Russian writer Aleksandr Solzhenitsyn points out what is wrong in every human heart, saying, "If only it were all so simple! If only there were evil people somewhere insidiously committing evil deeds, and it were necessary only to separate them from the rest of us and destroy them. *But the line dividing good and evil cuts through the heart of very human being.* And who is willing to destroy a piece of his own heart?" (my emphasis).[15]

---

[14] C. S. Lewis (1971) *The Four Loves*, Mariner Books. See https://www.cslewis.com/
[15] Aleksandr Solzhenitsyn (1973) *The Gulag Archipelago 1918–1956*, Harper & Row. See
https://www.goodreads.com/author/quotes/10420.Aleksandr_Solzhenitsyn

The answer to our problem

But the wonderful news is that God is personally invested in the state and health of our hearts and will not leave us to fend for ourselves. Instead, his strategy is to *move in*:

> For this reason, I kneel before the Father…I pray that out of his glorious riches he may strengthen you with power through his Spirit in your inner being, *so that Christ may dwell in your hearts through faith*. And I pray that you, being rooted and established in love, may have power, together with all the Lord's holy people, to grasp how wide and long and high and deep is the love of Christ.
>
> Ephesians 3:14–18 (my emphasis)

Yes, God wants to live in our hearts. He wants his ways to live there too: "Write these commandments that I've given you today on your hearts" (Deut 6:6 MSG). As well as living in our hearts, his desire is to heal our hearts and even give us new ones: "He heals the broken-hearted. And binds up their wounds [healing their pain and comforting their sorrow]' (Ps 147:3 AMP); "I'll give you a new heart, put a new spirit in you. I'll remove the stone heart from your body and replace it with a heart that's God-willed, not self-willed. I'll put my Spirit in you and make it possible for you to do what I tell you and live by my commands" (Eze 36:26 MSG).

Replacing our hearts? Is God going to perform major heart surgery on us right here on the kitchen table? No, I have a better analogy for how God wants to restore our hearts. It has less to do with butchery, and more with baking.

A lesson in bread making

Have you ever been in a kitchen when fresh bread is baking in the oven? What is it with the smell of baking bread? It's so inviting, so good. It's one of those smells – like freshly cut grass or a cool ocean breeze – that makes you breathe in deeply and say, "It is well with my soul", as the old hymn goes. Perhaps bread smells so good because deep down we recognise it as a staple, a life-giving food.

Jesus described himself as the 'bread of life'. "I am the living bread that came down from heaven. Whoever eats this bread will live forever. This bread is my flesh, which I will give for the life of the world" (John 6:51).

Imagine the scene in your kitchen (perhaps with your mouth watering slightly, if you're thinking of that fresh bread smell). Imagine that Jesus turns to you and asks: how soft is your heart towards me? Is your heart like freshly made bread dough? Will you be pliable in my hands? Will you allow me to knead you, stretch you, pull you in every direction I please to achieve my purposes in your heart?

His questions to us are not because he doesn't know the answers. They are always for our benefit, for us to ask the questions of ourselves. Perhaps you already feel like God is pounding you on his prep table. Just like any good baker, God wants to soften our hearts so that we become what we were originally meant to be. We need to trust him while he pounds us. We will need patience when God puts us in his 'proving drawer' where he leaves the dough to rise – when we feel put aside, or unseen. The rising process is a waiting process; it cannot be rushed. It takes as long as it takes, and the dough can do nothing in or of itself to speed it up.

The kneading and the proving are the times when we wrestle in our faith. We wrestle as Jacob did; we long for the blessings of God, for our ministry to take off, for healing to come in our bodies, emotions or relationships – or even a miracle to happen. And yes, it does feel like a struggle, especially those proving times when we are purposely put aside, feeling overlooked, unimportant or uninvolved. Oh, how I struggle with that, don't you? The longing to speak, to be seen, to be heard, to be significant, to just get on and do what I want.

Then, even when we are taken out of the proving drawer, brought back to the prep board and laid before him again, is he gentle with us? Often the answer is no! Our life, just like the dough, needs to be 'knocked back' – all the air seemingly knocked out of us. But we can only trust that he knows what he is doing more than it feels. If we allow him, he will hold us, mould us, and then leave us to rest for a second time.

Finally, just as we think the process is over, he puts us in the oven! In effect, he lights a fire in our hearts. Just as the heat of the oven changes dough into bread, so we are transformed by the power of the Holy Spirit living within us.

The process seems mysterious – all this pounding, waiting and firing – but what's the result? Bread. Life-giving, nutritious, delicious bread. Creating something so delicious takes a lot of work. A life that's been kneaded, proved, and fired brings forth a life-*giver*. As bread is to be eaten and enjoyed, our lives are meant to be shared and give life to others.

The kitchen in your life house is to be a place of creative activity, not some sterile, clinical room where everything is shiny but has never been used. The kitchen of our heart will sometimes be a hot and messy place. There will be stirrings, and what the Bible calls 'siftings' or times of testing; but what amazing progress will be made in the renovation process when you can say you "love the LORD your God with all your heart *and* mind and with all your soul and with all your strength [your entire being]" (Deut 6:5 AMP). Your life house may not have some great big farmhouse-style kitchen yet, full of life and love at the centre of your home – in fact, you may feel that the heart of your kitchen is just a single hot plate and a sink – but that's all you need to start. Remember what was said about the rebuilding of God's temple: "Who despises the day of small things (beginnings?)" (Zech 4:10 AMP, abbreviated).

Now that the work on your heart has begun – and a delicious smell is wafting from the oven – shall we carry on to another room?

RESTORATION REFLECTIONS

Choose one of the scenes below, then close your eyes and ask God to guide your imagination as you picture it. You might find it helpful to write down or draw what you saw in your mind's eye afterwards.

- You are a lump of dough on a floured board, waiting to be kneaded. Jesus is ready, apron on and sleeves rolled up. He looks at you with love in his eyes and asks: "How soft is your heart towards me? Will you be pliable in my hands? Will you allow me to knead you, stretch you, pull you in every direction I please to achieve my purposes in your heart?" What do you say to him? Be honest in your reply.

- You are a lump of dough that has been left sitting alone in a bowl all night to 'prove'. Jesus is nowhere to be seen. How do you feel? Call out to him. He comes into the kitchen and picks you up. Ask, "Why have you left me here for so long?" Tell him how you feel. What does he say? How does it feel to hear his answers?

TALK TO THE ARCHITECT

Heavenly Father, thank you that you love me so much and that your love is perfect in every way. Help me to have a soft heart towards you, and to not resist the restoration process you have planned for my life.

Thank you, Jesus, that even though there may be times I've felt stretched or overlooked, I know you're changing me to be all that you intend me to be. Help me to be patient and to trust you, even if I can't see or understand what you are doing. Amen.

CHAPTER 7
COME DINE WITH ME

If you have let Jesus into the heart of your home, his restoration of your life house has begun. Your kitchen is being repaired as we speak.

Your invitation

But as you look around the kitchen, you realised that Jesus himself has disappeared – and in his place stands a massive, shining angel. This mighty being is offering you a golden envelope in his outstretched hand, your name written on it in shining script. What do you do? Go on – take the envelope and open it. If you do, you'll find the following invitation inside…

You
....
Are cordially invited to dine with
THE KING
Come take your place that was chosen especially for you before the beginning of time.
Come eat. Come drink. Come have your fill.
There is always more than enough.
Come sit a while in his glorious presence and let your soul be satisfied.
Come as you are.

What do you think? Will you say yes? Trust me – it will be the best invitation you've ever accepted.

Let's imagine you turn to the angel and nod. On that signal, he strides across the room and begins to swing open two enormous bronze doors – into a room you didn't know you had. Through the doors you glimpse a soaring ceiling, dripping with diamond chandeliers, and a vast table clothed in snowy linen. The dining room of your life house has been prepared ahead of time, and Jesus is waiting for you to join him for a feast.

The first time I thought about meeting with Jesus in this way – as an invitation to dine with the King – I felt completely unworthy. After all, this picture is real. Jesus *is* royalty, and we *are* invited to sit and eat with him (Rev 3:20). In my case, I thought the angel must have the wrong person – perhaps someone else by the same name? But – "Oh, you of little faith!" as Jesus would say. Not only are we worthy to come, but Jesus *wants* us to come.

As you enter the room, you may worry that you're underdressed for such a place. But remember what the invitation said: "Come as you are." The King has already provided you with his own special garments. As you glance down, you realise you're wearing the crimson red cloak of covering that he gave you up on the roof. So you are dressed exactly right for the occasion. And your place is easy to find: it already has your name on it, reserved for you. It's the only place setting there is – apart from Jesus', right next to it. This is your seat at the high table, and it's just you and him.

Despite this grand table that seems never-ending – rich and opulent with its gold cutlery and serving plates, and brilliant crystal glassware – here you can feel completely at home. It's strange, but it's as if you're having a quiet supper with someone you love. This is how it feels to eat with the King.

Take your time, there's no rush – oh, and you may want to check the back of the invitation. There is a little note that says…

This invitation lasts a lifetime
Come every day!
My table is always ready for you.

You are chosen. You are invited by name. You are even provided with the right clothes. But it's your choice. In Jesus' story of the king who invites everyone to the wedding banquet (Matt 22:1–4), many refused to come. How will we respond to that daily invitation? Will we consider time with Jesus a chore, or a privilege?

Eating the scroll

Here comes that angel again, this time with an ancient scroll in his hands – it's the menu. If you're still staring at everything with your mouth open, don't worry about closing it – you'll have plenty to eat before you know it. You may even find yourself eating that scroll! But what does all this food you're being offered represent?

This food and drink is God's word, and it's designed to satisfy the hunger and thirst of every human heart and soul. His words in the Bible aren't simply there to be looked at. I've often said that I can just look at a cream cake and put on weight – sadly, however, my excess weight has come not from looking at cream cakes, but eating too many of them. With God's words we are to take them into ourselves as spiritual nourishment. We are to savour and digest them, as the only food that can truly satisfy and grow us spiritually.

> "Everyone who thirsts, come to the waters; and you who have no money come, buy grain and eat. Come, buy wine and milk without money and without cost [simply accept it as a gift from God].'
> Isaiah 55:1 (AMP)

His words are not just nourishing – they 'taste' good, as we read in one of Ezekiel's prophecies:

> 'as I opened my mouth, he gave me the scroll to eat, saying, "Son of man, eat this book that I am giving you. Make a full meal of it!" So, I ate it. It tasted so good—just like honey.'
> Ezekiel 3:3 (MSG)

Whether it's a quick snack of a single verse, or a seven-course tasting menu from a whole book of the Bible, we are all encouraged to "taste and see that the Lord [our God] is good; how blessed [fortunate, prosperous, and favoured by God] is the man who takes refuge in Him" (Ps 34:8 AMP).

And if taking in God's word is like a meal, it can't just be a one-off. It has to be daily. Even the Lord's Prayer says, "Give us today our daily bread". Both physically and spiritually we need to eat fresh food every day. When the Israelites were in the desert for forty years the Lord fed them with manna. He told them not to store it up, but rely on him to provide fresh manna from heaven every day. In the same way, we are to take in God's word every day. Some of us try to exist on old food, perhaps sentences we learnt long ago in Sunday school, as our only spiritual source. But just as the Israelites discovered, if you try to store up manna it doesn't keep – by the next morning it's riddled with maggots. You need to come daily to the King's table, and eat fresh food again and again.

Everyone eats, but for us as individuals, the time of day, the amount of food, and the way we eat it will all be different. It's just the same when it comes to eating spiritual food. However, the start of the day is crucial. I'm a big believer in eating a proper breakfast, although I often struggle to find the time for it – and likewise it can be hard to find time to sit down in a quiet place and read God's word every morning. But 'eating with Jesus' at the start of a new day is vital. While breakfast is important physically, fuelling us and starting up our metabolism after a night-long fast (hence 'break fast'), time spent taking in God's word is equally important. It sets us up for the day spiritually.

However, what I actually love is brunch – a much later, fuller version of breakfast – and this is mirrored in my spiritual meal times. The time of day that I find I am at my best is around 10.00am and usually involves at least two cups of coffee. I can spend a good two hours in the morning reading, journaling and praying – enjoying whatever the Holy Spirit has on his menu for me that day.

"That's all very well for you, Mandy," you might be thinking, "but I just don't have the luxury of time to do that every morning, with my kids or work schedule."

And in reality, I can't do this every day either. Sometimes all I have the capacity for is a quick glance at my daily devotional Bible verse, like a snatched slice of toast, as I'm out the door with a full day of errands ahead of me. And that's okay. Even though Jesus' dining table may be groaning under the weight of countless delicacies waiting for us to taste, he is also the Take Out King! His Spirit goes with us wherever we go. We can be sustained in simple ways – saying his name in our minds, recalling a recent Bible verse, arrow prayers of "Help!" and "Thank you, Lord." There are now daily Bible reading apps for smartphones so you can snatch a moment to read when you're out, like your lunch break (or bathroom break) at work. Some people, however, find the best time to read the Bible is last thing at night, after the kids are in bed or the main chores of the day are out of the way.

But whenever we find the time, we can then eat until we are full, and be thankful that he is the one who truly satisfies the hunger of our souls.

Gasping for a drink

What about a drink to go with your meal? As I sit here writing, I'm enjoying yet another cup of my beloved coffee. I can happily go from a couple of frothy cappuccinos in my morning quiet time to a super strong espresso at the end of an evening meal – via a few too many coffees in between. I love the stuff. But the trouble with coffee is that it dehydrates, rather than rehydrates. I've also been told that when we feel hungry it could mean we're thirsty but don't realise it. I think this is true of me; drinking enough water to keep my body hydrated is something I'm still learning to do.

Once, on the other hand, I drank water straight from a mountain stream. It was clear, fresh, ice-cold water that tasted like nothing I've ever had from a tap. Unlike coffee, it quenched my thirst straight away. This is the spiritual truth about Jesus. Being with him is like drinking water from a mountain stream, straight from its natural source. When we read and drink in God's message our spiritual thirst is satisfied, because it comes from the only source of 'living water': Jesus.

> "Now on the last and most important day of the feast, Jesus stood and called out [in a loud voice], 'If anyone is thirsty, let him come to Me and drink! He who believes in Me [who adheres to, trusts in, and relies on Me], as the Scripture has said, 'From his innermost being will flow continually rivers of living water.'"
>
> John 7:37–38 (AMP)

> "Jesus answered her, 'Everyone who drinks this water will be thirsty again. But whoever drinks the water that I give him will never be thirsty again. But the water that I give him will become in him a spring of water [satisfying his thirst for God] welling up [continually flowing, bubbling within him] to eternal life.'"
>
> John 4:13–14 (AMP)

Jesus' offer of living water is always there. But like me and my thirst for dehydrating coffee, we often run after – physically and spiritually – the things we believe will satisfy, while overlooking the one who really can satisfy. We are no different to the Israelites of the Old Testament. The prophet Isaiah said to them:

> "The Lord will guide you always; he will satisfy your needs in a sun-scorched land and will strengthen your frame. You will be like a well-watered garden, like a spring whose waters never fail."
>
> Isaiah 58:11–12

But this offer wasn't good enough for them, leading God to lament,

> "'My people have committed two sins: They have forsaken me, the spring of living water, and have dug their own cisterns, broken cisterns that cannot hold water"
>
> Jeremiah 2:13 (AMP)

Now, as then, we often believe we know how to satisfy our own thirst – but only end up drinking dirty, polluted water. For instance, there's the temptation to have an affair. We could be seduced by the exciting attentions of a work colleague who seems to fulfil our need to feel loved and significant. What we're likely to get in return – as people so often do – is the bitter taste of a damaged relationship or even a broken family.

Do you feel parched, as if you've been living in a desert? Drink in God's message – it will revive you. God keeps offering us living water every day to refresh and restore our souls:

> "The [Holy] Spirit and the bride (the church, believers) say, 'Come.' And let the one who hears say, 'Come.' And let the one who is thirsty come; let the one who wishes take *and* drink the water of life without cost."
>
> Revelation 22:17 (AMP)

When we come to Jesus and drink from his well of love, acceptance, significance, purpose and peace, all the areas of our life can begin to benefit, by being replenished and restored. A long-term relationship that was once dry or bitter can be transformed and renewed. What was once dead can become vibrantly alive again, all because we chose to believe Jesus' word to us.

If you need any more convincing that Jesus calls us to eat and drink with him, remember the most important meal in the Bible. At the last supper before his crucifixion, Jesus said to his disciples, "I have eagerly desired to eat this Passover with you before I suffer" (Luke 22:15). He told his followers that whenever they eat bread and drink wine they should do so in remembrance of him – hence the practice of Holy Communion, Eucharist or breaking bread that the Christian church has carried out ever since. We can join Jesus in that meal, not only at church, but every time we read and meditate on the Bible passages that describe it.

There is a banquet laid out for us every day in the Bible. The word of God nourishes and strengthens our inner being. It comforts and guides. It teaches and disciplines. It sets us free and gives us joy. It keeps us from sin and protects us. It shows us Jesus and so much more. We can be thankful, my friend, because we can say: "You prepare a table before me in the presence of my enemies. You anoint my head with oil; my cup overflows" (Ps 23:5).

By now I hope you are loosening your belt and wiping your mouth on one of the embroidered linen napkins, stuffed with good things like a Christmas turkey. Which reminds me of one our family's most famous stories…

The Christmas turkey

It was our very first Christmas in Basel, Switzerland, after we moved there following the path of Keith's career. Being English, it seemed only natural that we should have a roast turkey for Christmas dinner. So in early December I started the hunt for the perfect bird.

Having been to the local supermarket and not seeing either fresh or frozen turkeys on display I began to panic. In a frantic conversation with my neighbor, who spoke great English, she told me that I could in fact order turkey from the supermarket – I just had to tell them what I wanted.

So, off I went a week before December 25 on my mission to order our bird. As I'd only just started to learn German, I'd written down exactly what I wanted to order. With much trepidation, I stepped up to the meat counter, where a smiling butcher inquired how he could help me. I said I wished to order a turkey please.

"French or Swiss?" he replied.

That threw me straight away as I didn't know I'd be getting a choice – or what the difference was. But being loyal to my host country, I replied that I would like a Swiss bird. He then asked when I wanted to collect it.

"Christmas Eve," I confidently replied in my best German, as I'd got the answer written down.

Finally, he asked me how big the bird should be. I discreetly checked the weight I required by counting out the numbers on my fingers behind my back. Eins, zwei, drei, vier, fünf, sechs, sieben, acht, neun, zehn, elf.

"Elf," I proudly responded.

"Elf?" he said with a puzzled look on his face.

"Yes, elf," I returned.

"Really elf?" he questioned a second time.

I stopped in my tracks and frantically counted on my fingers, this time in full view of the confused-looking butcher.

"Yes," I said, "that's what I want, elf kilos for four people, two adults and two children!" Now the man stopped in *his* tracks. He looked me up and down slowly, scratching his head. "Okay," he said, "if that's what you want…" and he gave me the receipt for my order.

That evening I told Keith about my success in ordering my first Swiss turkey for Christmas. I was so proud of myself – one of my first hurdles living in a foreign land, overcome with ease. The fateful December 24 arrived, and amid all the preparations I sent Keith out to collect the prize bird. I heard the front door slam, marking my husband's return, and happily shouted out to him, "Have you got the bird?"

"Have I got THE BIRD?!" was all I heard before a massive 'thud' came echoing from the kitchen.

I raced towards the ominous sound – only to see what appeared to be a plucked baby dinosaur sitting on the kitchen counter.

"What's that?" I exclaimed.

"It's the darn turkey you ordered," Keith replied, out of breath from having to carry the thing home – but more importantly out of pocket, having had to fork out a small fortune for said monster.

I just stood there, transfixed by the sight before my eyes.

"That's not what I ordered," I said.

"What did you order, then?" Keith asked.

"Well," I began, "all I asked for was an eleven…"

And then penny dropped. What I had meant to order was an eleven-pound bird, but what I'd actually ordered was an eleven-*kilo* bird, which equates to around twenty-two pounds! Ah, no wonder the poor butcher looked so bemused. A twenty-two-pound turkey to feed four people, and two of them just kids! Well, he did look me up and down a few times, and as I'm a well-proportioned girl he probably thought, "Hey, who am I to know how much these people eat?"

My moment of being 'lost in translation' has been shared countless times with our friends, who relentlessly poke fun at me now about anything turkey-related.

However, getting my kilograms confused with my pounds is like God's word – you always get more than you bargained for. You might read it to learn one thing, but discover so much more. God can take a seemingly simple truth in scripture and open it up, taking our understanding and experience of Jesus' love to deeper and deeper levels. Even a single word can fill us up, just like our monster turkey!

You may be wondering what happened to that bird. Well, Keith had to cut both legs off to squeeze it into our standard-size Swiss oven. But to date, it was the best turkey we've ever tasted. And we were eating the frozen leftovers till Easter!

Fancy dining with the King? Go on, open that invitation. He might even be serving turkey, you never know…

RESTORATION REFLECTION

Choose one of the scenes below, then close your eyes and ask God to guide your imagination as you picture it. You might find it helpful to write down or draw what you saw in your mind's eye afterwards.

- You are standing in the kitchen of your 'life house'. A huge angel offers you a gilt-edged invitation to dine with the king. Using the invitation's words from the chapter above, read what it says, putting your own name into it. Will you accept? How do you feel?

- You sit down at the table beside Jesus. He greets you with a smile. When you're ready, turn to him and ask, "Jesus, why did you ask *me* to eat with you? What do you think about me?" What does he say?

TALK TO THE ARCHITECT

Lord Jesus, you have prepared a banquet table especially with me in mind, filled to overflowing with good things from you. Forgive me for the times I have turned down your invitation to eat with you, or tried to drink from empty wells. Thank you that I can come and dine with you whenever I want.

Holy Spirit, help me to always come to Jesus to receive everything I need to sustain my life and satisfy every thirst or hunger I will ever have. And in your time, fill me up so that streams of your living water flow from within me out to others in need. Amen.

CHAPTER 8
ROOM FOR ALL THE FAMILY

Here we are in the next room of your life house. Why don't we sit down for a bit? Just relax on the sofa a while. I could pop the kettle on if you like. I see you've got some photos on the mantelpiece – is that your family?

Keith and I both come from families with three children, and our own is the typical nuclear family: two parents, two children, one home. We have two daughters, Georgia and Sydney, and over the years, we've had various pets – a tank with a couple of goldfish, Grace and Petal the guinea pigs, and now Benson our bearded collie. This is our family, although Keith and I have recently become 'empty nesters'. Our girls have now both moved out to their own apartments and we find ourselves rattling around a big empty house. At least one advantage is that the house is mess-free (apart from our own).

However, and I can't believe I'm going to say this – sometimes I miss the mess. The mess of my girls' stuff all over the place spoke of us, our family, our relationships, our home together. For the reality is this, whether we like it or not – where people are, there will be mess. And 'messy' describes well the whole jumble of personal interaction we call relationship.

Loving relationships

Relationships are at the heart of our God. Christians believe in a triune God: Father, Son and Holy Spirit. Some believe that Christians worship three gods, but God is not one of three – he is three distinct persons in one. The Father is not the Son but is God, the Son is not the Holy Spirit but is God, the Holy

Spirit is not the Father but is God. God lives in relationship with himself. Each part of the godhead is in relationship with, and glorifies, the other. The only way I can begin to understand the trinity working in relationship is by looking at my own life. I know what it is to be relational as a mother, and at the same time to appreciate what it is to be a daughter and a wife – yet I'm still me, Mandy.

Confused? Yup, me too. The trinity is still something of a mystery to us, despite biblical scholars trying to get their heads around it for centuries – and I don't intend to expound on it here any further except to say this: God is into relationship. He loves us, and longs to be in loving relationship with us. God *is* love (1 John 4:8). He longs to restore all the relationships within our life house – our relationships with each other – and he does this through our love relationship with Jesus.

You might be thinking, "That's all very well and good – I can understand loving God because God is love, but it's all those others! I can't imagine loving *them*. In fact, I can't stand the sight of some of them."

Well, that's the point of this part of your life house renovation. Here in the living room – or family room – Jesus wants to put in order all the mess of our relationships – and the more people there are, the more mess there's likely to be. What are relationships within your immediate family like? (I ask about family rather than friends at this point, because as the old saying goes, "You can choose your friends but you can't choose your family.") What does a 'family room' look like for you? Even if you live alone, this room can represent relationships with any family you have, past and present.

Who's in control?

When our daughters are at home, the lounge is where we gather together, perhaps to chat, watch TV, or listen to music. Although if my husband or either of my girls were to interrupt here, they would say that chatting and listening to music was *not* the focus of this room because our TV is permanently on, whether someone was watching it or not. And I'm ashamed to say that would be true. In fact, my family would also tell you that the TV remote control might as well be surgically attached to my hand.

But this leads me to ask you: who holds the 'remote control' in the family room of your life house? If Jesus walked into it right now and asked you to hand the control of your relationships over to him, what would you do?

I have known families who are seemingly never at peace. Their life houses are full of hatred and chaos, abuse and pain. Everyone is playing the 'controller', yet they are all victims of the mess they themselves help to perpetuate. They try in vain to either change or run away from their mess, yet they never seem to get anywhere. They just repeat the same behaviour, expecting a different result every time.

Does any of this resonate with you? Is the 'family room' in your life house ringing with shouts, insults or silent screams? Are you trying to control, change, or 'fix' the other members of your family, without success? And does part of you think, "Why on earth would Jesus set foot into this mess?"

A friend of mine tells me about a time early in her marriage when the noise in her life house family room was reaching screaming pitch. She and her husband were new parents, and each felt they were suffering more than the other from the burden of sleepless nights and endless housework. My friend, especially, was building up a head of silent resentment. She had the family remote control firmly in her hand and despite pushing all the buttons, her husband was not responding the way she wanted. One day, out on a walk together after an especially bad night, it erupted into a proper row. They both said things they later regretted, and my friend's husband stomped off, leaving her boiling with rage and tears alone in the middle of the park.

"At that moment," says my friend, "I suddenly became aware that I wasn't alone. Jesus was there. I could feel the peace and presence of his Holy Spirit, even in my angry state. We had been so rude and childish to each other, but Jesus wanted to be with me anyway."

That experience encouraged my friend to persevere with the relationship, to let go of resentment and attempts to control, and now it's stronger than she had ever dared to believe. Jesus had not been put off by her mess – and because she had let him in and accepted his help, her 'family room' is in good order.

So even if you feel surrounded by chaos – stop. Listen. Take a moment to be still. Can you hear Jesus over those silent screams? "Child," he says, calmly and gently. "I am the Prince of Peace. Will you let me help?"

The Prince of Peace, a title given to Jesus in Isaiah 9:6, is not just one of his names but part of who he is. Could this be the moment you let him help you? Will you let go of your circumstances and let Jesus take control? Can you choose to stop trying to change or fix any of your family members, but prayerfully leave them in God's hands? You are promised peace if you do:

> "And the peace of God [that peace which reassures the heart, that peace] which transcends all understanding, [that peace which] stands guard over your hearts and your minds in Christ Jesus [is yours]."
>
> Philippians 4:7 (AMP)

We are never left alone when we trust God to restore our relationships by placing them into Jesus' hands. The only person we can truly control is ourselves, and self-control is a fruit of the Sprit. Jesus promises that the Holy Spirit will be with us to manage the process no matter how long it takes or how difficult or messed up things have become. Jesus himself said this:

> "Peace I leave with you; My [perfect] peace I give to you; not as the world gives do I give to you. Do not let your heart be troubled, nor let it be afraid. [Let My perfect peace calm you in every circumstance and give you courage and strength for every challenge.]'"
>
> John 14:27 (AMP)

A house for all the family

Because our relational God is God of the family, we are never left on our own. Even if you have no earthly family or friends – and in that sense, you are alone in this world – God never intended you to be lonely: "A father of the fatherless and a judge *and* protector of the widows, is God in His holy habitation. God makes a home for the lonely" (Ps 68:5–6 AMP). Our relational God longs for his people to live in community – not only with himself, but with each other. We do this as Christians when we meet together. We meet not *at* church, but *as* church.

All the people that make up the body of Christ are in an eternal sense our family – we are tied together not by the blood that flows through our veins but by the blood of Christ that was shed for each and every one of us. The name of our church in Basel, Oikos International,[16] is a good example. The Greek word *oikos* can mean both 'family' in one sense and 'house' in another – so a 'house for all the family' if you will.

Followers of Jesus have always met in homes, and coming together as family is still important. Many people believe you can have a personal faith in Jesus without 'making it public' or meeting with other Christians. But in my view, this is not the type of faith that Jesus calls us to. While Jesus did take himself off to spend time alone with the Father, most of his earthly ministry was spent among the mess of people's lives, including the messy lives of even his closest friends. The New Testament tells us to keep meeting up:

> "and let us consider [thoughtfully] how we may encourage one another to love and to do good deeds, not forsaking our meeting together [as believers for worship and instruction], as is the habit of some, but encouraging *one another*, and all the more [faithfully] as you see the day [of Christ's return] approaching"
>
> Hebrews 10:24–25 (AMP)

But therein lies the problem for many of us, doesn't it? As our eldest daughter Georgia once said to me, "Mum, church would be okay if it wasn't for the people!"

I guess we all know what she means. Churches are full of people loved by Jesus, but not necessarily people we'd choose to spend time with. No matter what part of God's family you belong to – high church with bells and smells, middle-of-the road or just plain out there 'shaking in the Spirit' – there will

---

[16] Oikos International Church, Basel, Switzerland. See www.oikos-church.ch

always be the odd ones. The ones who are too loud or too intense. The ones who have too many problems. The religiously perfect ones. The over-emotional ones and the 'cold fish' who don't even say hello. The 'space invaders' who crowd you in, and the insensitive ones who have no filter between what they think and what they say. Oh, and in every church I've ever been in there is always, yes always, at least one 'weird church lady'. (And that's not forgetting *me*. Perhaps everyone else thinks I'm the weird one...)

Yet despite the reality of human nature, we must remember that Jesus loves us all and calls us to live in unity. He wants to bring us together:

> "In him the whole building is joined together and rises to become a holy temple in the Lord. And in him you too are being built together to become a dwelling in which God lives by his Spirit."
>
> Ephesians 2:21–22

He wants to bring peace, not just to us personally, but to our 'family room'. So we are urged to "make every effort to keep the unity of the Spirit through the bond of peace" (Eph 4:3). And it does take *every* effort. Because until the day Jesus returns, we will not find anything approaching a perfect church.

So many believers 'church hop' in the vain hope that the next church will be better. While they may have a multitude of reasons for doing this, with spiritual labels to justify them, often the real reason is that they've been hurt or offended in some way. Perhaps they felt ignored or overlooked, or just plain bored. And instead of allowing Jesus to confront them and heal the issue at hand, people leave – just like the end of so many romantic relationships. I've even heard of people leaving church because a new person had the audacity to sit in their seat. ("How very dare they!")

The fact is that even if I founded my own personal church, with myself as head pastor, worship leader, treasurer and administrator, it would be just as terrible as any church I've tried to leave behind. Why? Because *I'm* there! None of us are perfect. All our 'life houses' have messes and need restoration to one degree or another. If you move church for any and every reason, the next church will have the same types of people and you will have the same types of problem as the one you'd left behind. So, unless you physically move away from the area, or are 'called out' of your current church – in which case your leaders should send you off with their blessing – then it's best to stay put.

There's only one exception I can think of to this advice, but it's an important one – if you are being controlled or suffering actual abuse in your church. In that case, it may be necessary to remove yourself from the church and/or certain relationships for the sake of your own well-being; although with any decision you make, always consult Jesus first. He will guide you into a place of truth and peace.

Even in your imperfect church – or perhaps especially in your imperfect church – Jesus is in the business of repairing, restoring and fully renovating your life house right where you are now. Don't be tempted to put him off or to leave the work until another day. He will always use people and our relationships with them, however messy, to transform us.

Keith and I have had to learn this lesson after leaving the UK in 2001 to settle in Switzerland. Life, to start with, was strange. As well as being in a foreign country with an unfamiliar history and lifestyle, we'd left our friends, relatives and church family behind – and Swiss church culture was different to what we were used to. It would have been so easy for us to stay in an expat bubble, harking back to our old life back in England and not trying to make new relationships. However, God was the one who led us to this country, and the one who introduced us to our new church family. Over time he has helped us grow new relationships with other believers, friends and neighbours. I can't say it has been easy – nurturing relationships takes time and effort – but it has been well worth it.

If you want to use the vacuum cleaner, remember to plug it in

So, Jesus is getting to work, using messy people and our relationships with them to clean us up. But if it's down to other people and their messes, you may wonder, is the work ever going to end?

It's a good question. The issue is: *who* is doing the work? Life and relationships worked out by self-effort alone is a thankless task, just like tidying up after other people. You clean and organise one area, then turn around and find more mess. Or it's like trying to vacuum, only to find that the vacuum cleaner wasn't even plugged in…a pointless task indeed.

But it's what we all do at times, especially when we repeat the same relational mistakes we've made for years, and even repeat those made by previous generations. For instance, our marriages might be in danger of breaking up in the same way that our parents' marriages did – even though we swore to ourselves that when we got married we wouldn't repeat the mistakes our parents made.

The Bible talks about whole generations of families being affected by God's blessings or curses. In the middle of the ten commandments, Exodus 20:6 warns of three or four generations of punishment for those who 'hate' God, but thousands of generations of blessing for those who love him. Jesus is in the business of turning any curses into blessings – but only if we choose to obey, or in other words, if we come into agreement with what he says in action as well as words.

> "See, I am setting before you today a blessing and a curse – the blessing if you obey the commands of the LORD your God that I am giving you today; the curse if you disobey the commands of the LORD your God and turn from the way that I command you today by following other gods, which you have not known."
>
> Deuteronomy 11: 26–29

God wants to bless us and our relationships, not only with our physical families but our spiritual family too. Jesus can break the chains of generational curses on us and our families. For some, the process of breaking these chains may take a lifetime, for others they may be just one prayer away. But the first step is always ours: to agree with him. God is a master of family reconciliation, but it is only a work he can do *with our agreement*. He promises to: "turn the hearts of the fathers to their children, and the hearts of the children to their fathers [a reconciliation produced by repentance]" (Mal 4:6 AMP).

We are never forced to do what God says. Our God is a loving God and his relationship with us is based on love. We can choose to agree, or not, with the work that Jesus wants to do in the family room of our life house.

I leave you to consider the choice God set before his people before they entered his promised land; this can be our choice too, if we resolve to let him restore our life and relationships:

> See, I set before you today life and prosperity, death and destruction. For I command you today to love the LORD your God, to walk in obedience to him, and to keep his commands, decrees and laws; then you will live and increase, and the LORD your God will bless you in the land you are entering to possess.
> But if your heart turns away and you are not obedient, and if you are drawn away to bow down to other gods and worship them, I declare to you this day that you will certainly be destroyed. You will not live long in the land you are crossing the Jordan to enter and possess.
> This day I call the heavens and the earth as witnesses against you that I have set before you life and death, blessings and curses. Now choose life, so that you and your children may live.
>
> Deuteronomy 30:15–19

RESTORATION REFLECTIONS

Choose one of the scenes below, then close your eyes and ask God to guide your imagination as you picture it. You might find it helpful to write down or draw what you saw in your mind's eye afterwards.

- You are in the family room of your life house, sitting next to Jesus on the sofa. You are showing him an album of family photos. Introduce Jesus to each person in the album, and tell him how you feel about him or her.

  Do you have any unresolved conflict with this person? If so, what is it? What does Jesus say about him or her?

- You are in the family room of your life house, sitting next to Jesus on the sofa. You hold the remote control. It represents your attempts to control the most important people in your life.

  Jesus says, "Can I have that? Can you hand over control of these relationships to me?"

  What do you say in reply? Be honest. If you can, give it to Jesus, and ask him to give you the gift of self-control instead. Receive his peace.

TALK TO THE ARCHITECT

Lord Jesus, thank you for all the people that are in the family room of my life. Where there is conflict I'm sorry for my part in it – please forgive me. I choose to forgive those who have hurt me in any way – I give them to you. Please forgive me for the pain I have caused to others and in so doing help me to let go of the pain I have carried.

Holy Spirit, I ask that you help me every day to maintain peaceful relationships with those around me. Heavenly Father, I ask that you bless all my relationships and bring healing and unity in Jesus' name. Amen.

CHAPTER 9
AND NOW DOWN TO BUSINESS

Onwards, my friend, to the next room in need of repair! Turning the handle and pushing the door open, I now present to you – the study. This is room represents our thinking, learning, planning and organising: in other words, our minds.

Your home office

You might find it difficult to imagine such a grand room as a study (or even a home office) in your life house; and perhaps you don't have this room in your actual home. Nonetheless, both your home and your 'life house' will have a place where you keep important information. So a study room you definitely have, even if it's just a battered brief case stuffed with various documents.

As for me, I would love to tell you that my office at home resembles an Oxford professor's room, with high ceilings, oak-panelled walls and a large impressive desk laid with everything I need to organise my life. In reality, our little office is a corner just off the lounge containing a shelving unit, a desk and a small filing cabinet which tends to get dumped with a whole variety of things that really belong somewhere else. But whatever the size or state of our offices at home, this room in our life house provides a good analogy for our minds.

If your mind is the home office in your life house, what does this room look like? How is it furnished? Jesus has a plan to remove every piece of flimsy, flat-packed, self-assembled furniture – our rickety, insubstantial thoughts and poor decision-making abilities – from our studies. He wants to replace them with fine, solid, handcrafted pieces, individually designed for us, that reflect a sound mind and the ability to make good choices.

The human brain, some would say, is the peak of God's creation. It is beautiful in its complexity, consisting of 100 billion neurones, each containing anywhere from 1,000 to 10,000 synapses. It is thought that the brain is thirty times faster than the best supercomputers. But Scripture is clear that we don't know everything:

> "Call to Me and I will answer you, and tell you [and even show you] great and mighty things, [things which have been confined and hidden], which you do not know *and* understand *and* cannot distinguish.'
>
> Jeremiah 33:3 (AMP)

Or as Woody Allan puts it, "If you want to make God laugh, tell him your plans!"[17]

Have you been led astray by your own reasoning, no matter how logical you thought it was? You might know the saying, 'Where the mind goes, the man follows' (Prov 23:7). This can even happen in following the news. When was the last time you checked the source of a so-called fact reported on television or in an internet post? There have been few periods in history when we've needed to be aware of propaganda in the media like we do today, with the term 'fake news' in everyday use. Regardless of our political, religious or socio-economical world-views, it's becoming increasingly difficult to know for sure what is true, what is harmless fiction, and what is downright evil.

Having come into relationship with God, our minds need to be restored and renewed to follow him:

> And do not be conformed to this world [any longer with its superficial values and customs], but be transformed *and* progressively

---

[17] Woody Allen – see https://www.goodreads.com/quotes/87478-if-you-want-to-make-god-laugh-tell-him-about

changed [as you mature spiritually] by the renewing of your mind [focusing on godly values and ethical attitudes], so that you may prove [for yourselves] what the will of God is, that which is good and acceptable and perfect [in His plan and purpose for you]

Romans 12:2 (AMP)

It's wise to seek wisdom

So, if Jesus wants to renew our minds, what does this look like?

Let's start with what it doesn't look like.

It is neither neurolinguistic programming nor cult-led mind control. Nor is it 'positive thinking.' Having a positive mental attitude to life will get you a long way, but only God can transform your mind. It's not even about being intelligent. There are millions of people all over the world who consider themselves highly intellectual – some have a high enough IQ to join MENSA's club for the intellectual elite. But even the most intellectual among us don't necessarily have much wisdom – and it's *wisdom* we need to have minds like Christ.

The great King Solomon knew this – on becoming ruler of Israel he prayed, "Give me wisdom and knowledge, that I may lead this people" (1 Chron 8:10). God answered his prayer spectacularly; not only did Solomon have an enviable knowledge of facts, but he had astonishing wisdom to make godly decisions.

So how do we get wisdom? Can it be found by studying and learning? No – knowledge and study aren't enough to renew our minds – not even Bible study. Religious people have studied the Bible for millennia, but not all of them have gained wisdom. Our studies are not to be about just getting and storing knowledge:

> "It's written, I'll turn conventional wisdom on its head, I'll expose so-called experts as crackpots. So where can you find someone truly wise, truly educated, truly intelligent in this day and age? Hasn't God exposed it all as pretentious nonsense? …the world in all its fancy wisdom never had a clue when it came to knowing God."
>
> 1 Corinthians 1:18–21 (MSG)

Knowing God, not just facts, is the key. Our studying is to be like an intimate marriage relationship – it should lead us into a closer walk with Jesus, and a greater desire to know him more. Jesus had strong words on this matter for the 'learned' teachers of the law:

> "You study the Scriptures diligently because you think that in them you have eternal life. These are the very Scriptures that testify about me, yet you refuse to come to me to have life."
>
> John 5:39–40

So *knowing* God through relationship is one facet of wisdom; another is *fearing* him: "The fear of the LORD is the beginning of wisdom, and knowledge of the Holy One is understanding" (Prov 9:10). The fear spoken of here is not being afraid of God, cowering in abject terror; but having a reverential awe for who Jesus is as the son of the living God, and what he has done for us in our salvation. This is the wisdom that renews our minds and is an essential part of restoring our life houses.

We are told,

> Through [skilful and godly] wisdom a house [a life, a home, a family] is built, and by understanding it is established [on a sound and good foundation], and by knowledge its rooms are filled with all precious and pleasant riches.
>
> Proverbs 24:3–4 (AMP)

This is a wonderful vision of the restoration work that Jesus has in mind for each of us.

The mind of Christ

The apostle Paul makes a staggering statement: "Who has known the mind of the Lord, so as to instruct him? But *we have the mind of Christ*" (1 Cor 2:16). Somehow, we are to have the mind of Christ, and know his thoughts.

Can our mind really be like God's? Even among humans there are different ways of thinking. Take, for example, the difference between the Greek (Western) and Hebraic ways of thinking. Greek thinking, which has influenced us most in the West, is based on abstract thought – we view the world through our minds alone. Whereas the Hebraic way of thinking is much more holistic, using all five senses – a much more 'hands on' approach than cold hard logic.

Even between men and women, we think differently to one another. My South African friend Amanda Buys puts it this way: it's as if men's brains are shaped like waffles, with each life activity separated into its own little square. Whereas women's brains are like balls of spaghetti, each strand overlapping and influencing all the others, everything interconnected with everything else. No wonder guys don't understand the gals in their lives! In fact, I have my own theory. I tell Keith that I think at the speed of light and he thinks at the speed of sound. Before you guys slam my book shut, the point I'm jokingly making is that you can't compare these different speeds of thinking, because they use two completely different wavelengths.

So it's no surprise then that God tells us:

> I don't think the way you think. The way you work isn't the way I work...For as the sky soars high above earth, so the way I work surpasses the way you work, and the way I think is beyond the way you think
> Isaiah 55:8–9 (MSG)

No, we don't have minds as if we were God; but we can know his thoughts and his wishes through Christ Jesus. We can know what is on his mind, what he is thinking about us and his plans for us. Jesus said:

> "But when he, the Spirit of truth, comes, he will guide you into all the truth. He will not speak on his own; he will speak only what he hears, and he will tell you what is yet to come. He will glorify me because it is from me that he will receive what he will make known to you."
> John 16: 13–14

Of course, it's not always easy to know which of the many thoughts we have every day might be God's thoughts. To try to make sense of this and understand how he is guiding me, I use what Nicki Gumbel (developer of the Alpha course) calls the five CSs. They each describe a way that God might speak to us. The 'convicting spirit' is when we feel the Holy Spirit speaking to our spirit, often a deep inner 'knowing' within us. 'Commanding scripture' describes the Bible speaking to us about a subject or situation. 'Counsel of the saints' is the advice or confirmation we receive from other Christians. 'Common sense' speaks for itself – often our intuition or gut feeling. Finally, 'circumstantial signs', while not worth much on their own, often confirm the other ways God has spoken to us.[18]

Furthermore, when we spend time with Jesus in prayer we can know what he thinks and feels about the awful injustices in this world. You can know his plans to help the poor and disadvantaged, not just in far-off lands but those in your own home town or even street. It was listening to the Holy Spirit, and feeling his pain, that led me to volunteer to work with women in Basel's red light district (see Chapter 14). As God renews the study room of your life house you can start to fulfil your personal role in bringing his kingdom to earth today, helping to answer the prayer, "Your kingdom come, your will be done, on earth as it is in heaven."

Out with the old…

However, our enemy the devil wants to whisper lies to us and deceive us. Do you have negative, destructive thoughts you can't get rid of? Maybe you're in a pattern of judging yourself or others, or feeling anxious about things that you know, logically, are not true – but your mind plays tricks on you?

We must refuse to believe what those thoughts say, and take hold of what Jesus has to say instead. With God's help, we can pin down what is untrue – perhaps "I'm a failure" or "God can't be trusted". Then we can replace this with the truth of Scripture, such as "I can do all things through Christ who

---

[18] Nicky Gumbel (2010) *Questions of Life*, Alpha International

strengthens me" or "God loves me; Jesus died for me". In this way we learn "to take our thoughts captive" (2 Cor 10:5). God's plan to restore our life house means out with the old, in with the new – we cannot simply add what Jesus thinks to a study already filled with our old ways of thinking. "Such a person is double-minded and unstable in all they do" (James 1:8). But we are to know the truth and the truth will set us free (John 8:32), renewing our minds in the process. To go deeper into the subject of taking our thoughts captive I recommend the Freedom in Christ course or similar Christian discipleship resources.[19]

Jesus is the expert when it comes to restoring the study room in our life house. But he doesn't just throw Bible verses at you like a pile of technical specifications, leaving you with no idea where to start, yet alone how to understand any of them. As with the whole of your restoration project, Jesus will take you by the hand and walk you step by step through each part of his plan. We can only grasp his thoughts through daily relationship with him anyway: not just day by day but hour by hour, minute by minute. We are to focus on Jesus, breaking an old habit by focusing on making a new one. There are also many great books that can help you through the process of God renewing your mind – a classic that has helped me is Joyce Meyers' *Battlefield of the Mind*.[20]

And remember that you are a work in progress. He knows exactly where you are in your rebuilding programme. And as Joyce Meyer famously put it, "I'm okay and I'm on my way",[21] and "I'm not where I need to be but thank God I'm not where I used to be".[22]

I don't want to stress you out if you hated school, and break out in a sweat at the thought of sitting a test – but our 'study' is to be tested. Teachers use tests to check that we've learnt what we were taught, and God is no different.

---

[19] See https://www.ficm.org, including their free downloads
[20] Joyce Meyer (2008) *Battlefield of the Mind*, Hodder & Stoughton
[21] Joyce Meyer - see www.joycemeyer.org/Articles/ea.aspx?article=im_ok_and_im_on_my_way
[22] Joyce Meyer - see https://www.goodreads.com/quotes/794007-i-m-not-where-i-need-to-be-but-thank-god

And just like any human teacher, God will be silent in times of testing. If you're going through such a time right now, remember this: God may not be speaking right now, but he hasn't left you alone in your study room either. He is right by your side, waiting till you've sat this test. And don't worry – if you haven't passed, you can take the class again, and again – until you realise that he is the only answer you will ever need anyway.

Dodging responsibility

Your home office might be the place where you go through your accounts and make decisions about spending. I'm the first to admit that I'm very good at spending money, but not so good when it comes to saving it – so if you saw me sitting in my home office checking my bank account you might hear some interesting language! In the same way, your mind is where you make choices – and take responsibility, or not, for their cost.

I heard a preacher ask recently: "What are you spending your life on?" He went on to say that every single human being who ever existed has spent their life on something – and even if it was spent just sitting on the sofa, it cost something. Our lives are valuable and not to be wasted.

Jesus knew there was a cost to those who would choose to follow him. He said:

> Anyone who comes to me but refuses to let go of father, mother, spouse, children, brothers, sisters – yes, even one's own self! – can't be my disciple. Anyone who won't shoulder his own cross and follow behind me can't be my disciple. "Is there anyone here who, planning to build a new house, doesn't first sit down and figure the cost so you'll know if you can complete it? If you only get the foundation laid and then run out of money, you're going to look pretty foolish. Everyone passing by will poke fun at you: "He started something he couldn't finish."
>
> Luke 14:27–30 (MSG)

Jesus paid the ultimate price for us. Are we willing to pay whatever price it takes to follow him? While we come under his protection as his own precious possessions, we also come under his authority. That makes us responsible to him for our choices, responsible to answer for what we spend our life on. Your life house is just that: yours. When you meet Jesus face to face at the end of this life, he is going to ask you how you spent it. What will you say?

We can't dodge this responsibility. Here is a way God taught me that lesson as I journaled one day, continuing the theme of the fun fair.

The dodgems of responsibility

I catch up with Jesus, panting slightly from my jog from the last ride. He is standing in front of the dodgems – an enclosed racetrack of bumper cars, colliding continuously with one another. Unlike the dodgems I'd seen as a child, this ride has a race track marked out, complete with lanes and a finishing line. And as well as avoiding other cars, drivers have to dodge around the 'pillars of responsibility' in their path. I can make out the names on some of these pillars: 'Truth', 'Care for others', 'Honesty'. I definitely want to avoid those! This ride looks fun.

A whistle blows and the cars slow for new drivers to take control of the vehicles. Without waiting to see what Jesus thinks, I climb over the barrier, clamber into the nearest car and clutch the steering wheel with purpose.

Oh great! I'm in the driver's seat – just how I like it. Total control over the car, its steering, acceleration and brakes. Instinctively my foot hits the pedal and the car lurches forward. I start to speed up as I enjoy weaving around obstacles in my path. I swerve wildly around the pillar marked 'Truth' and have my first collision with another car. Bang! The driver's name is on his helmet: 'Deception'. I've crashed my car into the consequence of my choice.

I shake myself to realign my jumbled thoughts and I'm off again, driving in the easiest, widest lane. The power of my pride surges through me and I'm pushed back into my seat by the force of the acceleration. I whizz past other drivers, my speed blurring the outlines of their cars like so many smudged bugs on my windscreen. I lose concentration. Thud.

"Did I hit something?" I ask myself. "Is anyone hurt? Surely not."

Anyway, it wouldn't have been my fault if they were! I don't stop to check; I swerve past the 'Care for Others' pillar and continue to race around the track. I have no concern for anyone else. I just want to win the race.

"You're driving in a race for rats Mandy!" Jesus shouts as I whizz past him for the umpteenth time. "You can't win the rat race. You may be in this world but you aren't of it!"

I take my foot off the accelerator and begin to slow down. As other drivers overtake me I consider the choices I've made in my life. This world tells me that it is my human right to control my own life – to choose everything, even life and death. But I'm reminded of something a wise woman once said: "Choice is a privilege and not a right". I know that I am created with the freedom of choice, but I've never really understood what a privilege it is. A wonderful gift, but one with such responsibility!

I am suddenly struck with fear. Now parked on the track, the responsibility to choose is too much for me to cope with. I'm paralysed by passivity. I reason that if I don't do or think anything, if I refuse to make any decisions at all, I won't get hurt or hurt anyone else.

Then, bang! Another driver shunts into the back of my car.

This time I'm injured. Whiplash grips my neck and shoulders with pain. "It's their fault," I cry, as I rub my neck, trying to ease it.

Jesus is by my side.

"Jesus," I moan. "I want to go home."

"I will take you home in a little while, Mandy, but you must allow me to drive."

I grudgingly accept, and slide over to the other side of the bench seat to let Jesus take control. He smoothly positions the car into the narrow lane I hadn't bothered using before, leading to the finish line where we can exit the track.

As we move off together Jesus shows me how to drive, carefully choosing the direction and speed. And those pillars? Well, as we approach one marked 'Accountability', he stops the car. Instead of being something I needed to dodge, it's a rest stop where drivers can fill their tanks with more of his Holy Spirit. As my little car is being filled with more Holy Ghost gas, I turn to Jesus and ask,

"Why do I always think I can do everything without your help? What I want

to do I don't do, and what I don't want to do, I do. I just don't understand."[23]

"You're not the only one who's asked that," Jesus says. "Remind me to introduce you to my friend Paul when you get home."

No, we can no longer dodge the responsibilities we have for our life houses. We are to spend time with Jesus in our 'home office' every day, studying his plans and his thoughts, and letting our Holy Spirit project manager show us what work he wants to accomplish in and through us today. As we move on, let me encourage you with this:

> Summing it all up, friends, I'd say you'll do best by filling your minds and meditating on things true, noble, reputable, authentic, compelling, gracious – the best, not the worst; the beautiful, not the ugly; things to praise, not things to curse. Put into practice what you learned from me, what you heard and saw and realised. Do that, and God, who makes everything work together, will work you into his most excellent harmonies.
>
> Philippians 4:8–9 (MSG)

---

[23] Romans 17:15–20

RESTORATION REFLECTIONS

Choose one of the scenes below, then close your eyes and ask God to guide your imagination as you picture it. You might find it helpful to write down or draw what you saw in your mind's eye afterwards.

- You are with Jesus in the study of your life house. On the desk is a stack of paperwork – your daily thoughts. You know that some are good to keep, but some are unhelpful and have no place in your mind. Say to Jesus, "Show me a thought that needs replacing."

  Does anything come to mind – something untrue you may have been believing about yourself, God or others? Or something ungodly, perhaps resentful or lustful? Whatever he shows you, write it down.

  If it's sinful, you can screw up the paper and throw it away – it is no longer yours. If it's untrue, you can declare that, and speak out the truth instead. Ask God to help you think of a Bible verse that captures the truth. For instance, "I declare that I am *not* worthless to God. I know that Jesus loves me and I am the apple of God's eye" (Zech 2:8). You may have to repeat this declaration daily until it sinks in.

- You are sitting at the desk in your study, a test paper turned face down and a pen in front of you. God is testing you – perhaps through an area of your life that's difficult at the moment. As you turn over the paper, you see what subject he's testing you in. What is it – Patience? Grace? Trust? Is it something you find easy or difficult? Jesus is sitting in the room, but he doesn't speak or look at you. What do you think he wants you to know?

TALK TO THE ARCHITECT

Heavenly Father, I have made wrong decisions and held wrong beliefs that have affected both myself and others in my life. I turn from them now – please replace them with your light and truth. Where my mind has been confused and messy, please bring order and peace. Lord Jesus, please forgive me where I have ignored or run from things I'm responsible for. Help me by the power of your Holy Spirit to keep a short account of my thoughts, and through your grace renew my mind daily. Help me to seek only your truth, and give me the wisdom to know what to do with it. Amen.

CHAPTER 10
BOUDOIRS AND BUBBLE BATHS

We are now standing outside the door of your life house bedroom.

I wonder what this room looks like inside. Is it dedicated to intimacy and rest, inviting and safe, with a warm, comfortable atmosphere? Or will you open the door to chaos, where even finding your bed is a stressful challenge? Well, whatever state your bedroom is in at the moment, it's your private space. Go ahead – go in and shut the door.

The bedroom is the one place where most guests to your house are not invited. Our bedrooms are usually our sanctuaries; places where we can go to be alone and escape from the push and pull of the world. It is also a private place, where intimacy begins.

It might then surprise you that Jesus is here now, gently knocking on your door.

Does that surprise you? Because Jesus is a gentleman, he would never force his way into your 'safe' place; but he still asks to be invited into your bedroom, even when you have already let him into your life house. And if you think about it, why should you be surprised? Jesus calls us to intimacy with him.

Being vulnerable

Now that we've travelled together this far, you've probably realised that I'm very open about myself and my life. I've been given grace to be this transparent – and while I know it's not for everyone, it compels me to write as honestly as I can, in the hope that you won't feel alone in your faith walk. I hope that you'll be encouraged by hearing about my weaknesses as well as my victories.

If you need proof that God's given me grace for openness, Keith and I developed and ran a course for couples called 'Enriching sexual intimacy in marriage'. This may not sound like typical subject matter for churchgoers, but God clearly led us to create this course, including talking graphically about our own sex life. I was shocked that Jesus would ask me to talk on such an intimate subject. But he has restored our marriage to a point where we felt it only right that we tell others what he has done and can do for other marriages too. His work in our lives has given us this ability to be completely transparent.

In the words of one course attendee, our public vulnerability was "as if you crucified yourselves for us up on that platform". This man went on to say that hearing about our weaknesses and mistakes, and how Jesus was transforming our relationship, gave him fresh hope for his own marriage.

This may sound contradictory, but I actually find intimacy very difficult. I don't mean in my writing or day-to-day interactions with family, friends or people I meet. The intimacy I find most difficult is in communication with God, or to say it plainly – I struggle with prayer.

Let me try to explain. When you say the word 'intimacy' it almost sounds like 'Into me see!' And herein lies my struggle. Because when I speak to people, whether in writing, preaching or just having a chat, I can choose what I show of myself at any given moment. I can filter my preferences. I can hide my emotions and my motives. But that's not the case with God, is it? God sees everything! God sees me as I really am, and for me that knowledge is often so overwhelming that I feel completely vulnerable, stripped naked with nowhere to hide.

I know that prayer involves trust and knowledge, even on a basic level, that I am loved. And yes, I can say that I do trust Jesus and I do know deep in my heart that I am loved – but I still feel drawn into something more, something deeper and stronger than I have yet experienced in prayer – and I think this is what I pull away from. I'm tempted to run away rather than engage. Remaining in control is my default, and as Jesus said, my spirit might be willing but my flesh is weak (Matt 26:41). I often allow my flesh or my soul rule and override what my spirit is desiring to do, and that is to get closer to God.

Learning that it's okay to be vulnerable before God is the first step towards intimacy.

Being childlike

Remember the famous children's story by Hans Christian Andersen, 'The Emperor's New Clothes'? The vain king is hoodwinked by two 'weavers' into wearing what he believes is the best, most expensive suit of clothes ever worn – so special it's invisible to those too common to appreciate it. As the king parades past the crowds in his new 'suit', it takes a little boy to point out that the king isn't wearing anything at all. He's completely naked!

This story speaks to me, vain as I am, about the shallowness of my usual prayer life. A child could see right through the façade. This is one reason why I believe Jesus said we are to come to him as little children:

> For an answer Jesus called over a child, whom he stood in the middle of the room, and said, "I'm telling you, once and for all, that unless you return to square one and start over like children, you're not even going to get a look at the kingdom, let alone get in. Whoever becomes simple and elemental again, like this child, will rank high in God's kingdom. What's more, when you receive the childlike on my account, it's the same as receiving me."
>
> Matthew 18:2–5 (MSG)

There are crucial lessons for us all to learn when it comes to intimacy in prayer, and becoming like little children is right up there on the essential scale, a close second to being vulnerable. Young children have no shame when it comes to nakedness – or any desire to cover up how they really feel. They feel no vulnerability or need to hide themselves. The risk of shame is something we become infected with as we get older. This is something that Jesus wants to restore in us – that freedom of an innocent, unmolested childhood. Becoming like little children is the second step into true intimacy with God.

Being ourselves

The third essential key I've found to growing in intimacy with God is intentionally setting aside time to be alone with Jesus, when we can be real with him. No one is too busy for this – we are "too busy NOT to pray".[24] Our prayers can be an offering of our exclusive time and attention for God, wafting up to him like the incense used in the ancient Jewish temple. The Bible tells us that we are like an aroma pleasing to God (2 Cor 2:15).

However, in the same way that I find the smell of incense a little overwhelming and cloying – it seems to stick in the back of my throat – I sometimes feel that my efforts at prayer are like overly scented candles or oil filling the bedroom in my life house, masking unwanted odours. I sense this sometimes when my prayers become too full of religious jargon or when I'm not being truly myself, saying only what I think I should say rather than what's actually on my heart. But I've come to realise that this approach to prayer is wrong. Real, intimate prayer with Jesus does not mask anything, and is never cloying or stale.

No, if we pray on our own (so we are not tempted to put on a religious act) and talk to God from our true, unmasked selves, then our prayers are like the morning dew or the first glimpse of the sun rising. They are our intimate conversations with God, fresh every morning. Making time for God, especially alone at the beginning of our day, is such an intimate act – putting him before and above any other priority just as Jesus did. The gospels report many times that Jesus went away by himself to spend time alone with his Father, and Jesus wants us to mirror this in our own lives. We all too often fall into the trap of thinking that we prayed in church on Sunday or at the prayer meeting, and that was enough. Yes, there is a time and place for coming together as church and praying with others – but this should not become our sole experience of intimacy with God. In fact, all we really need is to close that bedroom door and risk being ourselves with him. This paraphrase of Jesus' words says it all:

---

[24] The title of Bill Hybels' classic book: Bill Hybels (1988) *Too Busy Not to Pray*, InterVarsity Press

And when you come before God, don't turn that into a theatrical production either. All these people making a regular show out of their prayers, hoping for stardom! Do you think God sits in a box seat? Here's what I want you to do: Find a quiet, secluded place so you won't be tempted to role-play before God. Just be there as simply and honestly as you can manage. The focus will shift from you to God, and you will begin to sense his grace.

Matthew 6:5–6 (MSG)

Rest

When we become intimate with God an amazing thing happens: we experience true rest.

Clearly, the bedroom should be a place of rest. Our physical bodies need rest in order to function just as much as they need food and water. But rest can elude many of us. The all-too-many worries of daily life and the stresses of relationships and work can keep us up in the small hours, when our bodies should be in restore mode. And for some of us, the need for physical rest seems like an extravagance that only the idle indulge in. But what does God say?

For the Lord GOD, the Holy One of Israel has said this:

"In returning [to Me] and rest you shall be saved, in quietness and confident trust is your strength." But you were not willing.

Isaiah 30:15 (AMP)

How sad that Jesus offers us rest when we come to him, but so many of us refuse his help. I know how that burden of performance can weigh us down and rob us of intimacy with God. On top of work and family responsibilities, we can allow ourselves to be kept busy by church activities – and not always with the right motives. Sometimes it's to get others' respect or approval, rather than to serve God; or because we've elevated serving him above simply being with him. Jesus reminds us of this in these famous verses in the Bible:

Come to Me, all who are weary and heavily burdened [by religious rituals that provide no peace], and I will give you rest [refreshing your souls with salvation]. Take My yoke upon you and learn from Me [following Me as My disciple], for I am gentle and humble in heart, and you will find rest (renewal, blessed quiet) for your souls. For My yoke is easy [to bear] and My burden is light.

Matthew 11:28–29 (AMP)

Now while they were on their way, Jesus entered a village [called Bethany], and a woman named Martha welcomed Him into her home. She had a sister named Mary, who seated herself at the Lord's feet and was *continually* listening to His teaching. But Martha was very busy *and* distracted with all of her serving responsibilities; and she approached Him and said, "Lord, is it of no concern to You that my sister has left me to do the serving alone? Tell her to help me *and* do her part." But the Lord replied to her, "Martha, Martha, you are worried and bothered and anxious about so many things; but only one thing is necessary, for Mary has chosen the good part [that which is to her advantage], which will not be taken away from her."

Luke 10: 38-42 (AMP)

The rest God wants us to experience in the restored bedroom of our life house is like falling into the most comfortable bed you've ever slept in, where soft sheets surround you and you are held safe and sure, as the old hymn reminds us, in the 'everlasting arms' (Deut 33:27). God wants you to unburden yourself when you come to him – and to do that, shouldn't you take something off? We get out of the clothes we've worn all day when we get into bed – the formal suit we wore at work, or the sweatpants and T-shirt we wore looking after young children at home, or something in between – and put on comfortable night clothes, or maybe nothing at all. In the bedroom of our life house we can take off the uniforms of our usual roles and responsibilities, and simply be ourselves. Take off what hinders your intimacy and your rest.

Hang on – this room has another door! And someone behind it is calling your name…

Bubble baths

You've opened the door to an en suite bathroom, but all that greets you is a blinding bright cloud of warm steam and the sound of running water. And from the depths of the steam you can hear Jesus, calling: "Deep calls to deep in the roar of your waterfalls; all your waves and breakers have swept over me" (Ps 42:7). Can you hear him calling you? Will you go in? What awaits you if you do?

If this is making you nervous, don't worry – in a few short steps you're at Jesus's side, standing beside a huge enamelled iron bath tub with feet shaped like lion's paws. It is filled to the brim with hot, subtly scented water that is topped with massive pearlescent bubbles.

You might now be asking yourself, do I really need a bath? I'm not that dirty, am I? I think I smell quite nice. But the truth is that every human being needs a good scrub in this bath – as the Bible says, "all have sinned and *continually* fall short of the glory of God" (Rom 3:23 AMP) – even those people who look so good on the outside. Jesus had stern words for some of them:

> "'Woe to you, teachers of the law and Pharisees, you hypocrites! You are like whitewashed tombs, which look beautiful on the outside but on the inside, are full of the bones of the dead and everything unclean. In the same way, on the outside you appear to people as righteous but on the inside, you are full of hypocrisy and wickedness.'"
>
> Matthew 23:27–28

So, what do you think – is it time for your bath after all? Are you ready?

As you stand before Jesus he asks you to unburden yourself by taking off those clothes you've been wearing. As well as the 'uniform' of your daily life, he asks you take off that bad habit, attitude, or grudge you've grown used to because you have been wearing it for so long. It's only in taking it off that we realise how much it's been weighing us down. If your burden is so habitual that you struggle to undo it, don't worry. Let Jesus help you with the zipper. He is gentle and kind, ready to take away everything that separates you from God – for Jesus is the "Lamb of God who takes away the sin of the world" (John 1:29b).

This act of taking off dirty clothes is also known as repentance. It's as simple as acknowledging what is wrong, asking for forgiveness, and handing it over. Then it's not yours any more. There's no need to dwell on it, or keep on saying sorry, any more than you'd take a dirty shirt out of the laundry hamper and put it back on again. Once we've taken off those soiled clothes, Jesus doesn't air our dirty laundry for everyone to see, nor does he sweep it under the bath mat. He takes it and it's gone. Any mess we've made he washes away completely.

Now he offers you his hand to help you get in the water. Don't be alarmed that the water is as red as blood. It's his blood that "purifies us from all unrighteousness" (1 John 1:9). Jesus' work in the bathroom of your life house is to give you a deep clean. It will require your full immersion in his blood-red, but life-giving, water. Jesus is the only one who can do this. No religious preacher or teacher or adhering to a set of rules can get you fully clean. Blood-red water may not sound very cleansing, but you'd be surprised.

This chapter is the last I'm writing for this book (I don't tend to write chapters in order, but as the Holy Spirit leads). I'm sitting in the warm comfortable lounge of a spa hotel in the Black Forest in southern Germany. Keith and I have escaped for a few days, with the hope that I would finish writing this book, as well as have some intimate time with God and each other. As I write about God cleaning us, I'm reminded of this: "Soak me in your laundry and I'll come out clean, scrub me and I'll have a snow-white life," (Ps 51:7 MSG). Just as I lift my eyes from the keyboard, I look out of the window and guess what? It has started to snow!

The cleaning process Jesus has in store for us is holy and pure. Jesus' cleaning creates a 'down-to-earth' kind of holiness, like those snowflakes drifting slowly from the sky. Not a holiness that piously looks down on others, but one that comes down to where you are, raises you up and completely transforms you, as deep snow transforms a landscape – as different as day is to night and life is from death. The first time we are washed in this way is like the act of baptism – a declaration that God has not just cleaned us, but made a brand new person from the old:

> "We know that our old self [our human nature without the Holy Spirit] was nailed to the cross with *him*, in order that our body of sin might be done away with, so that we would no longer be slaves to sin."
>
> Romans 6:6 (AMP)

In the waters of our life house bathroom, Jesus not only wants to clean us, but begin the healing process: by his wounds we have been healed (1 Pet 2:24). And while he has miraculous, instantaneous healing in store for some, for many of us it's an ongoing process of coming into the bathroom every day and letting Jesus gradually heal us. Sometimes your bathroom may become an operating theatre, where deep inner healing takes place. It may involve delicate work that only Jesus, the most skilled surgeon, can do. Treating emotional wounds can be painful – perhaps a traumatic memory will come up, or you may find yourself weeping with deep grief over something he puts his finger on. But if Jesus is the surgeon, tears can be part of your healing. And one thing is sure: you *will* be healed in Jesus' name.

You may have wondered what I was doing all this time as I stood outside your bedroom door. Well, since I heard the bathwater running, I've been praying for you, talking to Jesus and asking him to heal you. This is something we all can do for our family, friends or even a stranger. As part of our intimate relationship with Jesus we have the privilege to stand in supporting prayer, asking God to heal another person. We ask him to come into another's life house and begin the clean-up process too.

Praying for others to be healed is not as difficult or complicated as I once thought. I used to think it was the exclusive realm of specially trained people with excellent prayer lives. I was wrong. My simple discovery came when Keith was due to have an operation on his knee. He'd been having a lot of pain, and the cause was confirmed by an X-ray and MRI scan as a torn meniscus. On the morning of the operation I was in the garden with Keith, and I decided on the spur of the moment to put my hand on his knee and 'say a little prayer' that it would be healed in Jesus' name. The surgeon told us, to our complete shock, that on opening Keith's knee he found a fully intact meniscus which didn't need any repair whatsoever!

Yes, Jesus heals. Sometimes instantaneously, sometimes over time, and sometimes mysteriously, in ways we don't understand. Sometimes people die without any healing, despite plenty of faith-filled prayer. But our faith is in what we cannot see, and trusts that in our heavenly home, sickness and pain do not exist at all – for by his wounds, *all* of us are healed. And if you are feeling a little discouraged as you have yet to experience or see healing then I'd say to you – keep on praying! Because when we pray then we may see healings happen, but if we don't pray, then we can be sure that we won't. But take heart, my friend – the promises to cleanse and heal us are in the 'now' and 'yet to come' reality that sits in the heart of God and cannot be taken from us.

Now I can hear the water splosh as Jesus offers you a hand out of that glorious bathtub. As promised, its blood-red water has left you perfectly clean. And even if this was your first time, you are invited to take a dip anytime you need. Jesus' cleaning, reviving waters are always available to you. Every day you will be like Peter, only needing to have your feet washed:

> Then he poured water into a basin and began to wash the feet of the disciples, drying them with his apron. When he got to Simon Peter, Peter said, "Master, *you* wash *my* feet?" Jesus answered, "You don't understand now what I'm doing, but it will be clear enough to you later." Peter persisted, "You're not going to wash my feet—ever!" Jesus said, "If I don't wash you, you can't be part of what I'm doing." "Master!" said Peter. "Not only my feet, then. Wash my hands! Wash my head!" Jesus said, "If you've had a bath in the

morning, you only need your feet washed now and you're clean from head to toe. My concern, you understand, is holiness, not hygiene. So now you're clean."

John 13: 6-17 (MSG)

Jesus cleansed us from sin once and for all on the cross, but he still invites us to come every day to the bathroom in our life house so he can wash off the daily grime of frustrations, stresses or conflicts that can hinder our holiness. At other times Jesus will invite you to come and soak in his presence…to do nothing but relax, lay back, spending time and receiving more from his Spirit. All you need do is strip off, jump in, and enjoy.

RESTORATION REFLECTIONS

Choose one of the scenes below, then close your eyes and ask God to guide your imagination as you picture it. You might find it helpful to write down or draw what you saw in your mind's eye afterwards.

- "Come and rest," says Jesus. He's in a chair right next to your soft, comfortable bed. Is it easy to climb onto the bed, or is anything holding you back? Does it feel lazy to have a rest? Does your mind leap ahead to everything you must get done? Or can you relax and let Jesus sing over you, as you rest in his Spirit?

- You are standing by the bath in your dirty clothes. What sins do they represent? Name each sin as you take it off and hand it to Jesus. Notice how he takes them without condemning you, and as soon as the clothes touch his hands they are gone.

  As you stand there, completely naked before him, how do you feel? What does Jesus say to you?

- Step into the bath and lie back in the warm, soothing water. Know that you are being cleaned from head to foot, and inside out. As you lie there, do you sense any need for healing, either physical or emotional? Ask the Lord to heal you. What does he say to you?

TALK TO THE ARCHITECT

Lord Jesus, thank you that with you it's safe to be completely vulnerable and childlike. I thank you that I can be completely myself with you, and that you know me intimately. Holy Spirit, help me take off any wrong attitudes or sin, including any masks I've worn, that would hinder me coming close to you. Heavenly Father, I thank you that I can rest in your arms and be cleansed and healed in Jesus' name. Amen.

CHAPTER 11
LET'S GET PHYSICAL!

So, how are you doing? Have you followed my exploration of our 'life house' chapter by chapter, or have you just joined us now, skipping to the chapter title that most takes your fancy? If so, that's fine – there is no fixed order to the way God restores our lives, although it may help to read the first two chapters so you know what this book is about.

In fact, if you have just joined us at this point, I'm intrigued to know what drew you to a chapter with this title. If you thought it was about sex, I'm sorry to disappoint you – this room is the gym!

Who cares about my body anyway?

Here we are – at the gym in your life house. This room is all about how you relate to your physical body. Let's see – is it well equipped and tidy? Or does it consist of a couple of dumb bells gathering dust in a corner?

To be honest, I'm shocked to find that I have so much to say on the subject of my body. In the planning stages of this book I'd considered not including this room at all. In my own ideal home, I'd rather have a spa than a gym – a room where I can be pampered, rather than one where I need to put in any effort. I'd even convinced myself that the years of ignoring my own physical health meant I had little or nothing to share on the subject. Yes, it would be the shortest chapter ever written. How wrong was I?

The truth be known, I'm the queen of procrastination. My motto could be "why do today what can be put off until tomorrow?" It's already February

– and while some wintry sunshine is cheering me up today, it's a time of year that usually says one thing to me: failure! You know what I mean if you too subscribe to the annual torture of setting unattainable goals every New Year, only to have 'fallen off the wagon', started smoking again, dumped the diet or mislaid that gym membership card by the start of February. Oh, the shame! All those good intentions to get fit and healthy, discarded like the jeans that are still too small to squeeze into. (For as long as I can remember, I've been watching my weight. Quite literally – I've just watched as the numbers on the bathroom scale have gone up and up.)

So – what, you may think, has this got to do with any holy renovation work? Well, one thing I've discovered is this: God is just as interested in your physical body as he is in your soul.

Early in my Christian walk I assumed for some reason that God wasn't so interested in my 'flesh' – and that was good, because I've got a lot of it. It was easy, suddenly, to become super-religious and disregard my physical self, wrongly believing that to be spiritual you must ignore the physical. I misread scripture and misused verses to confirm to myself that it was only my inner self that Jesus wanted to work on.

In my first book, *Gorgeous: Seeing yourself through God's eyes*, I wrote about my years of low self-esteem, being overweight, and my avoidance of one vital piece of scripture: "Do you not know that your bodies are *temples of the Holy Spirit*, who is in you, whom you have received from God?" (1 Cor 6:19). This verse was my nemesis. It haunted every little stumbling step of faith I took, my misunderstanding like a dark shadow trying to blot out the light of God's love for me. However, God himself began to reveal to me, through this same piece of scripture, that what I had despised for so long he in fact loved – even describing me as 'gorgeous'. He had a plan for even my physical body to be restored. Not just when I receive a new, resurrected, glorified body on Jesus' return one day, but for this life, now. One of the promises he gave me was: "I will repay you for the years that the locust has eaten…" (Joel 2:25a).

For me, so many years have been wasted either through yo-yo dieting or wishing I had a different body; but God promises restoration and this process starts, as with all that God does, with him loving us. On our tenth wedding anniversary Keith and I enjoyed a long weekend in Rome. I absolutely love art that depicts the naked human form – oil paintings, sketches and especially sculpture – and Rome is full of these. Wandering around inside St. Peter's Basilica, I marvelled aloud at how the sculptors were able to capture such intricate detail in bronze and marble: every soft curve, muscle definition or delicate vein crafted so carefully. In response I heard the Father say, "They got that idea from me, you know."

God loves his creation. He loves how he made you and me, and wants to teach us step by step not only to accept our bodies, but to love them just as he does.

Only recently I was reminded again of God's words to me. I was not expecting Jesus to revisit my 'gym room', but clearly more renovation work was needed. Coincidently, it was another wedding anniversary – our 29th – and Keith and I were visiting an exhibition of Cézanne's works in a museum in Basel. A pencil drawing in the artist's sketch book showed a voluptuous naked woman, reclining on a sofa. I was mesmerised; I loved it. And suddenly, to my surprise, Jesus challenged me again.

He said, "Mandy, ask yourself – why is it you can see the inherent beauty in this picture, yet when you look at yourself naked in a full length mirror you cannot accept your own beauty?"

My first taste of restoration was hearing God describe me as 'gorgeous'. But this next step in his renovation work was for me, not just him, to love and appreciate my body. It's only when we come to a place of loving self-acceptance that we can begin to partner with God and start actively caring for ourselves. This recent revelation has confronted me to make a choice; and I'm choosing, albeit slowly, to begin to love not only who I am, but my own body too.

How about you? Do you love and appreciate your own body? God loves your body – he made it, after all:

> For you created my inmost being;
> you knit me together in my mother's womb.
> I praise you because I am fearfully and wonderfully made;

your works are wonderful,
I know that full well.

Psalm 139:13–16

We've all seen documentaries about how amazing the human body is. From our outer skin with its many layers, to the very DNA of our individual makeup, we are astonishing. The fact that it's a masterpiece of God's creation is, in itself, a reason to love and care for it. But it's not the only reason – your body is a temple of the Holy Spirit.

Temples of the Holy Spirit

When you open the door of your life house and let Jesus in, his Spirit comes to live inside you – the actual power and presence of God's Holy Spirit in your physical body.

The Bible says you are a new creation:

> 'Therefore, if any person is [in grafted] in Christ (the Messiah) he is a new creation (a new creature altogether); the old [previous moral and spiritual condition] has passed away. Behold, the fresh and new has come!'
>
> 2 Corinthians 5:17 (AMP)

We are temples of the Holy Spirit; we need to look after these temples. And if we worship God in a church building, how much more should we worship him by caring for the bodies he gave us? Shouldn't we eat healthy food, exercise regularly and make sure we get enough sleep? Just as we wouldn't go into a church and dump trash everywhere, so it should be with our own bodies and health. Why do so many of us, myself included, care for our bodies less than we would take care of a church building? For it's us who God lives within, not any building made of brick or stone.

> Therefore, I urge you, brothers and sisters, by the mercies of God, to present your bodies [dedicating all of yourselves, set apart] as a living sacrifice, holy and well-pleasing to God, *which is* your rational (logical, intelligent) act of worship.
>
> Romans 12:1 (AMP)

On the one hand, the Bible sees our bodies as weak and transitory. It reminds us that we were made from the dust of the ground, to which we will return when our bodies inevitably fail. We are like grass: "All people are like grass, and all their glory is like the flowers of the field. The grass withers and the flowers fall" (1 Pet 1:24). Our earthly bodies, though "fearfully and wonderfully made" (Ps 139:14) are here today and gone tomorrow. But on the other hand, they are capable of containing great power, because they are designed to be the dwelling place of great holiness. I once heard Allen Hood, Associate Director at the International House of Prayer in Kansas City, wonder aloud in a sermon how it was possible that being filled by the Holy Spirit didn't blow our bodies to pieces. And how could it be that God, in the person of Jesus, came to earth in the vulnerable form of a human baby? I find it astonishing that God would so humble himself as to live in a human body – not just for his 30-odd years in ancient Israel but forever, in resurrected form.

I think it all comes down to the issue of respect and reverence. We should respect and even revere our bodies – not for their own sake, but out of respect for God. It's not about worshipping the 'body beautiful' as the world sees it, but worshipping this God who not only created our bodies, but lives in them by his Holy Spirit. Yes, love, care and respect; these are just a few of the tools by which Jesus does his renovation work in the gym room of our life house.

Discipline and Grace

If you think of the average gym, it tends to be very much an adult area. As you might have guessed by now I'm not an expert when it comes to gyms, and whatever specialist equipment they should have. I have on a few occasions visited these hallowed halls of fitness, and believe it or not I do have a little room in my own house that has actual gym equipment in it. However, my experience of visiting the gym is not one of childlike joy or pleasure. It always seems so serious and foreboding – I might even say torturous. It's a place where you need to have discipline and follow the rules. There are plans to be followed, a certain number of reps to be achieved, kilograms to be lifted or kilometres to be completed. Phew, just writing about it is getting me into a sweat! But – before we give up on this room – I have some great news.

As I said, Jesus loves our physical bodies. And to prove it, he has provided the perfect helper to guide and encourage us in the daunting process of renovation. The Holy Spirit has been given the special job (among many others) of being our *personal trainer*.

Confession time: other than the Holy Spirit, I have had a personal trainer. (I can't quite believe I've just written that. I had to stop typing to reread my own words). Now before you start thinking I'm some kind of health freak, I want to put you straight. I am probably – no, definitely – the unhealthiest person I know, and I know quite a lot of people. I am currently extremely overweight for my height. I find it difficult to walk up steep inclines without getting out of breath and needing my asthma inhaler – and don't even ask how fast I can run. Let's just say it straight: I'm unfit! Now you realise why I've tried to avoid writing this chapter.

What I can also say is that my personal trainer was truly a gift from God. Her name is Grace. She's a friend of mine. I'd known her for many years, and even though we don't run in the same friendship circles we would bump into each other from time to time. In fact, what I mean is that we'd see each other at church events, and Grace would give me what I can only describe as a rib-crushing hug. Now, I am a hugger. In fact, I believe one reason God made me was to give people much-needed hugs. But Grace gives *off-the-scale* hugs. Her hugs remind me of my grandfather Ted's – so strong they could take your breath away. Yes, this is my friend Grace. She is supremely physically fit. She has been a professional volleyball player and now works in the fitness industry. Grace is the fittest person I've ever met, and she wanted to help me.

One Sunday, while I was lounging on my sofa at home and merrily tucking into a giant chocolate chip cookie with a cup of tea, God spoke to me. It was a definite 'God moment'. I heard his voice, very clearly, as if he were just behind me speaking over my shoulder.

"Mandy," he said, "Ring Grace and ask her to help you with your health and fitness!"

One reason I know it was God speaking was my reaction. I got up from the sofa, went to the phone and rang Grace straight away. I didn't think about what I was doing – I just did exactly what he told me. After a quick and somewhat garbled conversation with her, I finished my call and sat back down on the sofa. Keith looked over at me as if to say, "What on earth was that all about?"

In the few silent seconds that followed I began to ask myself the same question.

You see, although Grace is a friend of mine, I'm just going to come right out and say it – she would be the last person on earth I'd ask for help with my physical health. The reason, as I'm sure you are wondering, is that Grace is *disciplined*. Oh no, not the D word! Yep, Grace for me is discipline personified. Now I know she wouldn't be so boastful of herself to say that – and of course she, like the rest of humanity, is not perfect – but if one thing can be said of Grace, it's that she lives a healthy, disciplined lifestyle. I would go so far as to say that she is 'hard core' when it comes to health.

I believe that God is a compassionate, merciful, kind and gentle God – and I would add that I believe he has a great sense of humour. He loves partnering with us in ways we would never choose for ourselves. I can just imagine him having a right old belly laugh, not at our expense of course, but with the glorious supernatural knowledge of what we will become – despite ourselves. You see, if I had stopped for long enough to think about what God had asked me to do, "Are you kidding?" would have been my reply to his instruction.

So, I met with Grace and explained how God had prompted me to call her. She asked me how committed I was to changing my life. She prayed for me, then invited me to my first gym visit in at least 25 years. Arriving at the gym I was shocked to discover that it wasn't filled with skimpily clad Lycra ladies as I'd imagined, but quite normal-looking people.

Grace had arranged a simple ride on the static bike. Easy, you might think. But what I had unrealistically thought would only be a five-minute cycle turned into 30 minutes of progressive resistance training. Well, I cried like a baby almost the whole time I was on it – yes, how pathetic! – while Grace prayed and sang over me. I puffed and panted and cried some more. My legs burnt with the effort and my knees ached.

"Oh Lord," I prayed, "help me!"

And he was helping – he had started the painful process of showing me how unfit and undisciplined I'd allowed myself to become. It took grace to show me that. Not only my friend Grace, but grace, the unmerited favour of God.

The Bible says, "Therefore, there is now no condemnation for those in Christ Jesus" (Rom 8:1). Just as Grace did not condemn me for my lack of discipline, but constantly encouraged me throughout the whole sorry session in the gym, in Christ we are not condemned. We are free to be transformed.

Thanks to this freedom, I'm now choosing to care for my gym room, my body. Jesus is helping me learn the restorative art of self-control and how to use the tool of discipline to achieve the changes he's planned for me. Whether we are 'fighting the flab' or doing anything else to care for our bodies, we need to understand that we're taking part in a cosmic battle between our spirits and our self-centred 'flesh'.

Paul put it very eloquently:

> 'For I know that nothing good dwells within me, that is, in my flesh. I can will what is right, but I cannot perform it. [I have the intention and urge to do what is right, but no power to carry it out.] For I fail to practice the good deeds I desire to do, but the evil deeds that I do not desire to do are what I am [ever] doing.
> Now if I do what I do not desire to do, it is no longer I doing it [it is not myself that acts], but the sin [principle] which dwells within me [[a]fixed and operating in my soul]'.
>
> Romans 7:18–20 (AMP)

This is the human condition, and it's very obvious to me when I try to discipline myself to exercise. Fortunately, just as Grace helped me in the gym, God's grace helps us in the battle with our bodies – through the Holy Spirit's fruit of self-control.

> For the flesh desires what is contrary to the Spirit, and the Spirit what is contrary to the flesh. They are in conflict with each other, so that you are not to do whatever you want. But if you are led by the Spirit, you are not under the law.
> …the fruit of the Spirit is love, joy, peace, forbearance, kindness, goodness, faithfulness, gentleness and self-control. Against such things there is no law.
>
> Galatians 5:17–18, 22–23

Could it be that self-control, the last in that list of the Spirit's fruit, is the most difficult to develop? And what practical aid does the Holy Spirit offer us? Well, whether or not you like the sound of this, the answer Jesus gives us is 'daily denial'. The world urges us to deny ourselves nothing, but Jesus told us to 'pick up our cross' and follow him. The amplified version of this verse clarifies:

> 'If any person wills to come after me, let him deny himself [[a]disown himself, [b]forget, lose sight of himself and his own interests, [c]refuse and give up himself] and take up his cross daily and follow me [[d]cleave steadfastly to me, conform wholly to my example in living and, if need be, in dying also].
>
> Luke 9:23 (AMP)

I can hear your groans from here. Yep, denying yourself is saying NO to self. It's not a case of us being in control, it's rather us choosing to control the self. Self-control and discipline involve making active, positive choices every single day. Sometimes the positive choices I make to look after my body may be as small as choosing to have a glass of water instead of another cup of coffee, or fetching something from upstairs myself instead of asking Keith – but the tiny steps of denying the flesh build us for the bigger challenges. And each choice is like exercise – the more you repeat it, the easier it becomes. But remember, when you fail, as we all inevitably will, our Lord's response is to comfort our souls: "Because of the Lord's great love we are not consumed, for his compassions never fail. They are new every morning; great is your faithfulness" (Lam 3:22–23).

A first step in God's renovation process is revealing the realities in our lives that we'd been trying to hide from. I learnt that day in the gym that I'd been in denial about myself: this room of my life house was in dire need of renovation. Not just a touch up here and there, as I'd vainly hoped, but a total transformation. The saying, "You can catch a disease but you can't catch health" is so true. I learnt that I'd need to develop and strengthen my levels of discipline and self-control – help that the Holy Spirit was offering me in the person of my friend Grace.

So here he stands with you now – your own personal trainer, pumped up and ready to start the restoration of your gym room. Are you ready to begin?

RESTORATION REFLECTIONS

Choose one of the scenes below, then close your eyes and ask God to guide your imagination as you picture it. You might find it helpful to write down or draw what you saw in your mind's eye afterwards.

- You are standing with Jesus outside the door to your gym room, looking through the glass door at what's inside. This room represents your physical body: what state is it in? How do you feel about it? Proud? Disinterested? Ashamed? Are you eager to go in and get training, or is anything holding you back? Tell Jesus how you feel. What does he say?

- You are standing in the middle of your gym room. All around you are different types of fitness machine, each representing different aspects of your physical health. Jesus is directing you to a specific one that you need to work on. What area of your health does it represent? How is Jesus saying you should use it?

TALK TO THE ARCHITECT

Heavenly Father you are the creator and everything you make is good. I thank you that every morning I can wake knowing that it is you who puts breath in my lungs, keeps my heart beating and loves me unconditionally. Please forgive me where I have mistreated my physical body and help me turn to your way of healthy living.

Lord Jesus I ask that you reveal to me the areas that need to change in relation to my health. Where I am addicted to either a substance or behavior or even relationship that is unhealthy for me, please show me and set me free.

Holy Spirit, please grow in me the fruit of the spirit that is self-control. Equip me with the discipline I need to live healthily and give me the grace to live the abundant life that is promised me in Jesus' name. Amen.

CHAPTER 12
WHAT ARE YOU LOOKING AT?

Now that you've worked up a bit of a sweat, take a break and consider the question Jesus is posing in the title of this chapter. He has placed a large mirror in front of you and invites you to take a long hard look at your reflection.

In the gym room of your life house, did you look around and dream of renovating it as one of those hi-tech, sophisticated gyms that 'beautiful people' use? You know the kind – fully equipped with expensive equipment, high-intensity lighting, and sparkly clean floor-to-ceiling mirrors…? They may look great, but remember: with all those lights and mirrors there is literally nowhere to hide! Does that idea make you wince? Are you afraid to look in the mirror Jesus is holding in case your eyes are drawn to all the faults you find in your body, or can you look at yourself and say, "I'm okay"?

I don't know about the 'body beautiful'. As I explained in the last chapter, I hadn't begun to think mine was beautiful at all until recently. Why do we, as adults, have so many hang-ups about our physical bodies? Young children don't – they accept their bodies just as they are. Little kids are oblivious to the world's judgement of skin colour and they don't attach any particular value to size. But as teenagers, while we try to cling onto our individuality, we are also desperate to fit in and look like our friends. And as adults, most of us conform to society's norms for how we should look – and those who don't are often seen as deviant and undesirable. Then in old age we can end up feeling that we've become ugly, irrelevant and invisible. How awful! We're not meant to be like a little row of houses that all look the same. That's one of the reasons I believe Jesus calls us to come to him as little children. We can come to him with open hearts and a complete lack of self-consciousness and learn to love what we see.

It's all in the eyes

Let's start with your eyes. How healthy are they? Jesus put it like this:

> Your eye is the lamp of your body. When your eyes are healthy, your whole body also is full of light. But when they are unhealthy, your body also is full of darkness. See to it, then, that the light within you is not darkness. Therefore, if your whole body is full of light, and no part of it dark, it will be just as full of light as when a lamp shines its light on you.
>
> Luke 11:34–36

When I read this for the first time I wondered what it meant for me, since one of my eyes is not healthy at all – as a child I spent a lot of time in London's Moorfields Eye Hospital, having been born with only 20 percent vision in my right eye. However, I learnt not to take this verse so literally. It's more about the way we look at the world around us; our renovation process means that we gradually start to see in new ways, seeing what Jesus sees. As the restoration process of our life house transforms us from glory to glory, it not only changes us to see our true selves – how God sees us – but also to see how God sees others. And the moment I start judging and complaining about others, Jesus puts up a mirror to bring the focus back to myself. He shows me my own selfish attitudes that need cleaning up before I ever get around to focusing on someone else's mess.

> 'Why do you look at the [insignificant] speck that is in your brother's eye, but do not notice and acknowledge the [egregious] log that is in your own eye? Or how can you say to your brother, 'Let me get the speck out of your eye,' when there is a log in your own eye? You hypocrite (play-actor, pretender), first get the log out

of your own eye, and then you will see clearly to take the speck out of your brother's eye'.

Matthew 7:3–5 (AMP)

So, what about you? Among all the wonderful things Jesus is known for, one is making blind eyes see. Could it be that he wants to heal your blind eyes today?

"Blind?" you might say. "I can see perfectly well, thank you very much."

We may have 20/20 vision physically, but how well can we see morally or spiritually? Do we see that a prostitute is the same as a victim of sex trafficking? Are refugees people fleeing for their very lives or just migrants we don't want to see in our neighbourhood? Are our eyes deceiving us? Perhaps, also, we are looking at things that damage us, but are in blind denial that they're doing us any harm.

And if our eyes' lack of health reflects what's going on in our hearts, how much darkness is there within us? Yet our restorer is gentle and kind to us. Even when we can't see what's in front of our own noses, the promise to us is this:

Beloved, we are [even here and] now children of God, and it is not yet made clear what we will be [after His coming]. We know that when He comes *and* is revealed, we will [as His children] be like Him, because we will see Him just as He is [in all His glory].

1 John 3:2 (AMP)

Windows on the world

Let's take a look at the windows of your life house. Unlike mirrors, windows offer us two perspectives: what we see out of them and what others can see of the inside. So how clean are they? My windows at home are often in desperate need of cleaning. Our dog Benson seems to love slobbering all over them as he looks out at the world going by, and they could be called 'streaky' at best, with a dull film of dust and grime that actually changes how much light comes into our home. Call myself a good Swiss housewife, I should coco! It wasn't until Keith cleaned them for me recently that I realised just how much my view of the outside world was blurred by all the dirt.

And here I pause, as Jesus asks for the second time, 'What are you looking at?' Are the windows of your life house in need of more than just a 'lick and a prayer', but a proper, thorough clean? Having a clear view of the world is very important to Jesus. What we see influences us. What we take in through our eyes can influence us positively, and unfortunately negatively too. This is what Jesus was talking about when he spoke about our bodies being filled with light. Are your windows allowing light or darkness into your life house?

The problem of porn

God sees everything – including pornography. "There is nothing concealed that will not be disclosed, or hidden that will not be made known" (Luke 12:2).

The pornography business is just that – a business. It's a multibillion dollar industry that can be accessed by a tap on a keyboard. And it's not just lads' mags anymore. The market for pornography specifically designed for women is increasing. If you're aware of *Fifty Shades of Grey* by E. L. James you'll realise how widespread acceptance of porn for women has become. I'll be frank – I've used pornography. It's not something I'm proud of. And young people today are exposed to porn in ways that could never have been imagined just thirty years ago.

Christian men are far from immune. In 2014, a non-profit organisation called Proven Men Ministries[25] commissioned a survey among a nationally representative sample of 388 Christian adult men. Of those who identified themselves as born-again Christians:

- 95 percent admit that they have viewed pornography
- 54 percent look at pornography at least once a month
- 44 percent viewed pornography at work in the last 90 days
- 31 percent had a sexual affair while married

---

[25] See https://www.provenmen.org/

- 25 percent erase Internet browsing history to conceal pornography use
- 18 percent admit being addicted to pornography (and another 9 percent think they may be).

Many people nowadays would disagree with me for saying that pornography is harmful. But the sad truth is that it's like dry rot, creeping into and invisibly destroying the fabric of our lives. The effects on men are becoming obvious, with increasing numbers experiencing serious relational difficulties and penile dysfunction. And money spent on pornography promotes the spiralling growth in prostitution, human trafficking and child abuse. If that isn't darkness, I don't know what is.

While porn isn't a problem for everyone, I suggest there are more than like to admit it – even to themselves. Remember Jesus' question: "What are you looking at? Has looking at porn influenced you so much that you now find yourself with sexual images of young children on your computer? Many thousands of people have been led into such deep levels of darkness that they no longer know how to escape. Whether they got there through morbid curiosity or an insatiable desire for greater and more depraved stimulation, the thought of being found out can be so overwhelming that there seems no way out.

However, there is a way to get out, and the Holy Spirit is here to show you how. He wants to rip all the dark influences out of your life, to scrub and polish the windows to your soul and brighten the lights of your eyes. He wants you to see Jesus. He wants you to not only see his light, but to shine it out – to be his light in this dark world.

One way we can help him do this is by making an agreement with our own eyes: "I made a covenant with my eyes not to look lustfully at a young woman" (Job 31:1). This is something Keith takes seriously. He's said to me, "It's not that I go about my everyday life with my eyes firmly shut – that's not practical, or actually the point. What I've determined is that, with the help of the Holy Spirit, I will not be led astray by what my eyes see. I choose to divert my gaze, change my focus and if necessary physically move myself until what I see is what Jesus wants me to see."

The Covenant Eyes[26] website is a great resource for anyone struggling with pornography. It helps you stay accountable to trusted friends about what websites you are visiting, as well as other practical help.

Making a 'covenant with your eyes' is not a silver bullet, but an everyday (sometimes seemingly every minute) commitment that we can make – and with God's help, our eyes and conscience will remain clear. If we slip up, immediate forgiveness is available. Freedom can be ours when we choose to cry out to the Lord. Whatever the issue that Jesus chooses to shine his light on, take heart, you are *not* alone.

The mess of media

Back in Chapter 8 I confessed to you my excessive reliance on television. I depend on it for noisy companionship in a house that feels too quiet, and perennial entertainment to numb an already bored mind. Yet what I watch on television and online have helped get the windows of my life house into a right old mess. Whether it was watching programmes that promoted the latest diet trend, or documented those obsessed with plastic surgery, I found myself fixated only on the physical – and what I saw in myself just didn't match up to the ideal. And this is where Jesus has me in my own personal restoration programme. He is confronting me with my own attempts at a clean-up, and quite frankly they have been pathetic. It's become a ride on the continual carousel of denial and guilt, as my weak will tries to change my viewing habits – feeling guilty one moment that I choose to watch particular programmes, but failing to stay away from trash 'reality' TV, then finding excuses for my continual consumption of viewing that's like stuffing my face with junk food.

"Oh Lord, help me," is my current cry. I need his help – that's the truth, pure and simple.

So, what about you? How is modern media messing up how you see the world? What smears and smudges might Jesus want to wipe from your life

---

[26] See www.covenanteyes.com/

house windows? Has being entertained visually become a problem for you as it has for me?

If you lived in the UK in the 1970s you'll remember Mary Whitehouse, a woman who always seemed to be in the news. She was very vocal about morality. Whenever there was bad language, nudity, violence or blasphemy on the screens or in the press, there she would be with another strong reprimand. She was lambasted for being a prudish killjoy.

Back then, I didn't really understand what all the fuss was about. She was depicted as a silly, annoying woman who was behind the times, and few people agreed with her views. Yet how things have changed since Mary's passing. Bad language has become part of everyday speech, and sexualised nudity not only commonplace but often celebrated as liberation. Violence of all types is so normalised, and seeing on-screen torture and murder has so numbed us, we hardly need warning captions anymore. Online or TV viewing can often leave us overwhelmed by a barrage of ideas or images that are unhelpful, or in some cases, downright harmful. And as for blasphemy – when the name of Jesus Christ is used as a grammatical exclamation (at best), need I say more?

But how can we close the door when the proverbial horse has already bolted? We can't, we need divine help. And as always, God the Father starts with changing the heart of one man or one woman through relationship with his son, Jesus – the only one who can clean up the mess we ourselves have made.

Being transparent

Another function of a window is, of course, to let others see in. Windows are transparent both ways. The definition of 'transparency' includes "having the property of transmitting light", "fine or sheer enough to be seen through" and "free from pretense or deceit".[27]

For me, being transparent involves me continually taking the risk to be

---

[27] See https://www.merriam-webster.com/dictionary/transparent

completely myself with others: the good, the bad, and even the ugly. It means not hiding behind the mask of who or what I think people want me to be.

How do you feel about letting people look in through the windows of your life house? Are you prepared to be transparent, and let others see who you really are? It's a good question to ask yourself, if you have the courage to answer it honestly. I reckon that most of us wouldn't like it if anyone could see in through our windows – but this is the life we are called to live. Jesus modelled for us a truthful life of integrity, humility and love, without pretence.

Living transparently means letting others see your mistakes, your sins and your weaknesses. It means no blinds or net curtains to conceal the view in through our windows. After all, covering our mistakes only multiplies them; think of institutions where child abuse carried on for decades because those in charge failed to blow the whistle. And just as a transparent institution lets others see when it has gone wrong and brings problems into the light, we as individuals need to do the same. Are you yourself when you're around others in church or at work, or like me are you tempted to hide your true self behind a mask, pretending you're something you're not? Are you accountable? Who do you confess your sins, problems and secret shames to?

First and foremost, we must take the step of being completely open with God himself. Even though he knows us better than we know ourselves, we still need to be real with him, confessing where we've gone wrong (again) and expressing our real feelings (like anger or fear) when we pray. It's a sign of our trust in him that we can be who we are, with all our failings, yet still be confident of his love for us.

Next, we are called to live transparently with those we say we love, those we are closest to. Again, it means admitting when we are wrong, and being honest about how we feel. It's tempting to lash out in anger and blame when a loved one has hurt us, but it's better to make ourselves vulnerable and say, "This is how I feel". (Relationship counsellors call this way of baring of our souls 'opening the kimono'). That vulnerability inspires others to be honest about their own feelings.

This is a hard way to live; sometimes we may get hurt or hurt another in our learning curve, but don't let that put you off. There is power in living a transparent life. Of course, it feels vulnerable, and it's natural to be afraid of ridicule. But when we choose to live openly and honestly by the grace of God, it becomes a powerful weapon in the Spirit. Nothing is hidden; there are no skeletons in the cupboard. No matter how hard the devil may try he just can't get his claws into us.

Before we move on to the next room, I'll leave you with this reminder. Just as I noticed how much brighter my house became when Keith cleaned my windows, so it is when Jesus cleans us up from the inside out too.

> This is the message we have heard from him and declare to you: God is light; in him there is no darkness at all. If we claim to have fellowship with him and yet walk in the darkness, we lie and do not live out the truth. But if we walk in the light, as he is in the light, we have fellowship with one another, and the blood of Jesus, his Son, purifies us from all sin.
>
> 1 John 1:5-7

RESTORATION REFLECTION

Choose one of the scenes below, then close your eyes and ask God to guide your imagination as you picture it. You might find it helpful to write down or draw what you saw in your mind's eye afterwards.

- You stand with Jesus in front of a full-length mirror. (Do this for real at home.) Take time to look at your reflection. Tell Jesus exactly what you see: describe yourself. Now say to Jesus, "What do you see when you look at me?" What does he say about you? How do you feel about what he says? How different is his description of you to what you said about yourself?

- You stand with Jesus looking out through your windows. Is the glass dirty or clean? Jesus asks you, "What are you looking at?" What is your response? What else is he saying to you right now?

TALK TO THE ARCHITECT

Lord Jesus, you made the blind see. Forgive me where I have refused to see your truth in my life. I ask that you heal me from any physical, emotional or spiritual blindness I may have, even blindness caused by my own self-righteousness. Help me Holy Spirit to see what you want me to see and give me that all-sufficient grace that will enable me to live a transparent life, in Jesus' name. Amen.

CHAPTER 13
STORAGE HOARDERS

Here we are, heading to the basement of your life house – or the garage – or wherever you tend to store your 'stuff'.

Personally, I'm not a hoarder. I'm not interested in collecting anything, although Keith might suggest that I have quite a collection of shoes and handbags (men just don't get the whole coordinated outfit thing). I'm one of those people who likes to have a place for everything and everything to be in its place. I actively enjoy a regular spring clean, ridding my house of anything unnecessary. Keith, however, is the complete opposite. He has his collection of precious vinyl under the stairs and his Star Trek memorabilia safely boxed away. He is a man who doesn't like to throw away anything that could feasibly be of any practical use in the future.

Who owns who?

Are you more like me or Keith? And how much stuff are you hoarding in your life house?

Storage hoarding has become a twenty-first century issue. Storage is business now. If you don't have enough room in your own home for all your belongings you can rent storage space for it. 'Storage Wars' is one of a whole breed of television programmes in which people bid for abandoned storage units, taking a chance that hidden treasures might be among the forgotten possessions.

And hoarding, in its extreme form, is a recognised mental health problem.

If the TV documentaries are to be believed, some people have filled their houses with so much stuff they can no longer use some of the rooms – bedrooms can't be slept in or bathrooms bathed in, because they are full of everything from piles of old newspapers to sacks of clothing. Their houses have become so full of rubbish that they've become serious fire hazards, and so cramped that normal the day-to-day activities are restricted.

But even if we don't suffer from this particular mental illness, it's likely that we've got more stuff than we need. And Jesus is in the mood for a spring clean.

If Jesus were to open up your garage or basement door today, what would he find? Would he open the door to see your pride and joy – a treasured trophy car, or perhaps an impressive wine collection? Most of us have something we treasure, something that would cause serious upset – or a call to the police – if it were taken from us.

But Jesus said:

> Do not store up for yourselves [material] treasures on earth, where moth and rust destroy, and where thieves break in and steal. But store up for yourselves treasures in heaven, where neither moth nor rust destroys, and where thieves do not break in and steal; for where your treasure is, there your heart [your wishes, your desires; that on which your life centres] will be also.
>
> Matthew 6:19-21 (AMP)

Jesus is more interested in the content of your character, and cleaning that up, than he is in helping you keep hold of all your wealth or possessions. Don't get me wrong; Jesus doesn't have a problem with possessions or wealth – it's what you do with what you have, and how you respond to God with it, that he's interested in.

As we stand at the top of the basement steps, or inside the garage door, Jesus' question to you is this: "Who has ownership of these things? Do you own it, or does it own you?"

There are two examples that Jesus gives as a warning to people with lots of possessions and wealth. In one, a successful farmer decides to build himself bigger storehouses so he can be free of worry about the future, and "eat, drink and be merry". God's response is "You fool! This *very* night your soul is required of you; and *now* who will own all the things you have prepared?" This farmer, Jesus concludes, was "not rich [in his relationship] toward God" (Luke 12: 20–21 AMP).

In the second example, a rich young man asks Jesus how to get eternal life:

> "If you want to give it all you've got," Jesus replied, "go sell your possessions; give everything to the poor. All your wealth will then be in heaven. Then come follow me." That was the last thing the young man expected to hear. And so, crestfallen, he walked away. He was holding on tight to a lot of things, and he couldn't bear to let go. As he watched him go, Jesus told his disciples, "Do you have any idea how difficult it is for the rich to enter God's kingdom? Let me tell you, it's easier to gallop a camel through a needle's eye than for the rich to enter God's kingdom."
>
> Matthew 19:17–26 (MSG)

In both stories, the farmer and the rich young man are materially well off. Some would even say 'blessed'. However, Jesus tells them that having either an abundance of possessions or money does not equate to being rich in God's kingdom. In fact, it is the complete opposite if wealth and possessions are the primary focus.

I think this quote from the actor Jim Carrey says the same thing in another way: "I think everyone should be rich and famous and do everything they ever dreamed of so they can see that it's NOT the answer."[28]

---

[28] See www.goodreads.com/quotes/1151805-i-think-everybody-should-get-rich...

Deep dark basements

"That's all very well," you might be thinking, "but these stories of wealth and possessions don't relate to me at all. I don't have a posh new car in my garage, my bank account is empty, and I don't own my home. So I'm not storing or hoarding anything that Jesus needs to clean up."

But God knows that we don't have to be rich to have a problem with possessions. Jesus' renovation programme reaches into every dark, dusty, cobwebbed nook and cranny. His vision reaches past what the human eye can see, into those areas in our lives that we thought we'd kept locked away. Our problem possessions might be emotional or spiritual; like feelings of shame, fear, or guilt, that we have hidden away and don't want to anyone to know about.

Switzerland is a very ordered country – I think that's why I love it so much. Even garages or storage spaces are kept neat and tidy. Our pastor Silvia spoke one Sunday morning about her desperate need to clear out her garage. It had become a dumping ground for anything and everything the family didn't need or use anymore, and so much stuff had accumulated that they couldn't even fit the car in. Silvia told us how ashamed she'd become of it – if the neighbours could see it, how terrible that would be! Then one fateful day she came home from a day out to see that the garage door had been left open and the whole street would have been able to see, all day, the mess that had been hidden away. What she had tried to hide in the dark was exposed to all her neighbours, much to her embarrassment (and our amusement).

Jesus can see right through our garage door. Jesus can even see what is stored in the basement – those deep, unconscious places where pain and abuse, brokenness and guilt are repressed and hidden.

In every horror film, there always seems to be a darkened basement that one of the characters decides to go into – and as I watch I find myself shouting, "No! Don't go down there!" (They always ignore me.) The creepy music builds as the person walks slowly down those creaky stairs, and the little candle or torch they were holding goes out…and I have to hide behind a cushion to not see what happens next. But Jesus isn't afraid of our dark basements or anything that lives in them: 'Even the darkness is not dark to You *and* conceals nothing from You, But the night shines as bright as the day; Darkness and light are alike *to You*' (Ps 139:12 AMP). Traumatic events that take place in childhood create some of the deepest and darkest places in our souls, and over time can become repressed, only to resurface with devastating effects later in life. However, the comforting truth is that Jesus is the only one who can not only bring light into that darkness, but release us from it too.

I've had an overwhelming fear of going to the dentist since the age of ten, when I woke up from the general anaesthetic in the middle of a procedure to remove four of my teeth. All I can recall of that moment now was blood, pain and my own screams. As the years passed, my trauma became so bad that even the sound of a dental drill or the vibration from the polisher caused me physical pain. This meant that I avoided going to the dentist for at least ten years – and when I had to go, the experience was horrendous. It wasn't until I was in my forties that I faced my fears, with the help of a wonderful Christian dentist called Karin. Karin prayed for me as I sat in the chair and, for the first time for years at a dentist's, I sensed peace and calm. Previously someone would always have to accompany me to appointments, staying with me even during a check-up, since just sitting in a dentist chair would cause me to shake uncontrollably. Now, after continued prayers and assurance that Jesus is always with me, I can go to appointments on my own without anxiety – Jesus has removed all those years of fear.

Does this story touch a nerve with you? Do you have a traumatic childhood experience that still affects you now? These can be the hardest memories to let Jesus into, but he can walk through those experiences with you and bring you healing. For severe trauma, this has to be done with great care and the help of an experienced Christian counsellor or psychotherapist. But there is nothing that God cannot bring into the light and heal.

So cleaning up is not a problem for Jesus, however deep and dark the room. But then what? Jesus not only wants to give your storage places a 'spring clean' – he wants to do an entire 'Spirit clean'. He tells this story:

> When an impure spirit comes out of a person, it goes through arid places seeking rest and does not find it. Then it says, "I will return to the house I left." When it arrives, it finds the house swept clean

and put in order. Then it goes and takes seven other spirits more wicked than itself, and they go in and live there. And the final condition of that person is worse than the first.

Luke 11:24–26

In other words, we can't just ask Jesus to clean us up and then show him the door, like some sort of domestic servant. No, we need Jesus to move in permanently, because he's the only one who can keep us clean and free. Chains that have held you captive in the dark places of your mind can be broken in his name. Even if you feel that under the surface, your life is like one of those horror movies basements right now, Jesus can get rid of it all – but he doesn't sweep it clean and walk away. He wants to stay, replacing all your 'stuff' with his gifts and treasures that will not only enrich you in this life, but supply you for your journey into eternity.

Gifts and treasure

Gifts – did that get your attention? Yes, God is good, and he has gifts to give. And I'm not just talking about the free gift of eternal life.

The Bible tells us that every member of the godhead gives gifts: Father, Son and Holy Spirit. Let's start with the Father.

Gifts from the Father

"Every good and perfect gift is from above, coming down from the Father of the heavenly lights" (Jas 1:17). Even more than the most generous earthly father, God longs to give his children gifts: "If you, then, though you are evil, know how to give good gifts to your children, how much more will your Father in heaven give good gifts to those who ask him!" (Matt 7:11). And what are these gifts? Some of them are listed here:

> 'Since we have gifts that differ according to the grace given to us, each of us is to use them accordingly: if [someone has the gift of]

prophecy, [let him speak a new message from God to His people] in proportion to the faith possessed; if service, in the act of serving; or he who teaches, in the act of teaching; or he who encourages, in the act of encouragement; he who gives, with generosity; he who leads, with diligence; he who shows mercy [in caring for others], with cheerfulness.'

Romans 12:6–8 (AMP)

Any of these gifts can be given to us as the Father decides, and they often relate practically to our everyday lives. I believe our individual gifts are often built into our DNA, and get released as we ask our heavenly Father to show us what they are. What do you like to do? What are you naturally good at? These can be pointers to gifts that Father God has already placed inside your life house. One of the most fulfilling things we can do in life is use our skills and abilities to the fullest, to achieve the purpose for which God gave them to us in the first place. And God doesn't give us gifts for purely our own benefit, but to help others. Do you have the gift of mercy – are you able to care for the sick or those in need? Or are you gifted in finance, and able to give where God directs? Go on, just ask him. He can't wait to show you what gifts he has stored up, ready for you to open and learn to use.

Gifts from the Son

What about Jesus' gifts? They're described here:

…[his gifts to the church were varied and] he himself appointed some as apostles [special messengers, representatives], some as prophets [who speak a new message from God to the people], some as evangelists [who spread the good news of salvation], and some as pastors and teachers [to shepherd and guide and instruct]

Ephesians 4:11 (AMP)

As your life house belongs to Jesus and you are therefore part of his church, then in his timing, and for his purposes, you too may receive a gift like one of these to build up his church.

Gifts from the Holy Spirit

> '…but to each one is given the manifestation of the Spirit [the spiritual illumination and the enabling of the Holy Spirit] for the common good. To one is given through the [Holy] Spirit [the power to speak] the message of wisdom, and to another [the power to express] the word of knowledge *and* understanding according to the same Spirit; to another [wonder-working] faith [is given] by the same [Holy] Spirit, and to another the [extraordinary] gifts of healings by the one Spirit; and to another the working of miracles, and to another prophecy [foretelling the future, speaking a new message from God to the people], and to another discernment of spirits [the ability to distinguish sound, godly doctrine from the deceptive doctrine of man-made religions and cults], to another *various* kinds of [unknown] tongues, and to another interpretation of tongues.'
>
> 1 Corinthians 12:7–10 (AMP)

So, what do you do when you get your hands on all those gifts he's stored up for you? It doesn't matter how you unwrap them – whether you are careful and methodical, or rip off the paper with wild abandon. The important thing is that you do open what God has for you and begin to use it. Don't just sit there looking at it, like it's a collector's item kept 'mint in box'. We should be the opposite of a storage hoarder. We are to keep giving away what God gives us, because we cannot out-give God. He always has more to give us than we could ever want or need. If you've received the gift of mercy, show mercy to another. If you have received wisdom, don't keep it to yourself. If you've been given the gift of prophecy, speak it out. We are no longer to be hoarders, but delight that God wants us to share, to give away what has freely been given to us.

A prophetic dream

The whole purpose for me of writing this book is to share with you what God has given me. I've been given the gift of encouragement, and my prayer is that this book is just that – an encouragement to you in your own renovation process.

As I mentioned right at the beginning, I often dream about houses. Sometimes God has also given me dreams that helped me to understand and open his gifts for me. The first time I had one of these prophetic dreams it involved houses. It happened right at the beginning of my walk with Jesus, when I'd never even heard of prophetic dreams. All I knew was that this dream was unlike any I'd ever had before. It was so vivid and detailed that I felt compelled to write down every detail, even drawing a picture of what I saw.

I open my eyes and I'm standing in a beautiful kitchen. It is light and airy; it has everything one would need to cook the most delicious food. I am standing by the sink looking out of the window into a garden. It's a lovely garden, but a bit plain, I think. In fact (I think randomly) that garden would make a lovely place for a swimming pool. I turn from the window and leave the kitchen. Strangely, the house I'm in is only a kitchen, with no other rooms…

I open the front door, and to my surprise I see that this 'kitchen house' has other buildings attached to it in a long terrace – and suddenly I have a key in my hand. I walk towards the terrace, a long row of quaint cottages with whitewashed stone walls and windows with four square panes of glass each, so that the frame makes the shape of a cross. I open the door to the first cottage and step inside. The front door is huge and old but doesn't creak as I expected it to. It has been well used, I can tell, but its hinges have been regularly oiled so it opens smoothly. Inside I discover that the cottage has only two rooms – one downstairs and one upstairs. To my astonishment, both rooms are stacked high with furniture. They are completely full. The furniture is old, but not unfashionable. It is fine antique furniture, old but cared for as if new. The sofas and chairs are covered with plush, red velvet and the tables and other items are made of all different types of wood – strong oak and deep mahogany, swirling walnut and rich cherry. I am overwhelmed by what I see. There is so much stored here I can't quite take it all in.

I leave the first cottage and explore the others in the row. I discover that there are seven of these cottages in the terrace, and the terrace is attached to the 'kitchen house'. All the cottages are identical in that they only have two rooms each, and all are full to the brim with beautiful furniture.

Then I wake up.

It wasn't until many years later, after we had moved to Switzerland, that I was reminded of that dream and was shocked to realise that it had become my reality. By this time, Keith and I were leading Alpha courses[29] – weekly sessions for those wanting to explore the Christian faith – for the English-speaking community in Basel. We originally ran the courses from our home, and I always cooked the meal that we shared with our guests: this was the kitchen in my dream. From my kitchen window, I would often look out over the neighbours' garden at the swimming pool they have there. I now call this pool my own, as we have since purchased our neighbours' house! I was personally involved with leading these courses for seven years (seven little houses). We ran courses twice a year, in the spring and in the autumn (two rooms in each house) and we always had exactly what we needed to run the courses; enough helpers and plenty of food (fine furniture in each house). Yes, God furnished all our needs indeed – I am still amazed to this day by the accuracy of that prophetic dream and the way God led me to use the gifts he gave me, working with him to fulfil his plans not only for my life, but for all those people who attended each course and who invited Jesus into their own life houses.

I've described my dream here because it's an example of God going before us, preparing everything we need to accomplish the work he's called us to partner with him in. You too have gifts and callings, waiting to be used in God's service; or perhaps you can look back over your life and see how some have already been used.

> 'For he delivered us and saved us and called us with a holy calling [a calling that leads to a consecrated life—a life set apart—a life of purpose], not because of our works [or because of any personal

---

[29] See more about the Alpha course at https://alpha.org

merit—we could do nothing to earn this], but because of his own purpose and grace [his amazing, undeserved favour] which was granted to us in Christ Jesus before the world began [eternal ages ago]'

2 Timothy 1:9 (AMP)

RESTORATION REFLECTION

Choose one of the scenes below, then close your eyes and ask God to guide your imagination as you picture it. You might find it helpful to write down or draw what you saw in your mind's eye afterwards.

- You are standing with Jesus in the garage of your life house. Around you are the possessions you prize most highly. What are they? Jesus says to you, "Do you own these possessions or do they own you? What if I asked you to give any or all of them away?"

- You are with Jesus at the top of the basement steps. Down in the dark are difficult or painful feelings you don't usually talk about to anyone. Jesus says, "Let's go down and look at these together." Take his hand and walk down the steps. As he shines his torch around, what do you see? What does he want to deal with right now? A painful memory may come to mind. Are you willing to let him heal it?[30]

- Jesus has presented you with a gift, beautifully wrapped. He watches to see what you do with it. When you're ready, take off the paper and open the box – what's inside? What natural or spiritual gift does it represent and how will you use it?

---

[30] For very traumatic past experiences, it is better to pray with a mature Christian friend you trust or a qualified counsellor. Helpful books on this subject include John and Paula Sandford (1985) *Healing the Wounded Spirit,* Victory House; Joyce Meyer (1994) *Beauty for Ashes*, Faithwords; Rev Joe Allbright and Rita Allbright (1997) *Liberating the Bruised*, Smooth Sailing Press, LLC.

TALK TO THE ARCHITECT

Heavenly Father, as I stand among the clutter in my life, I invite you to come and help clear away anything that hinders me from living freely the life Jesus died to give me. Change my priorities so that I may find joy and satisfaction in you, rather than material things that don't last.

Lord Jesus, I take hold of your hand, and in trust I give you permission to shine your light on anything hidden in the darkness in the basement of my life house. Take me step by step and show me what you want to deal with. Lead me into your light, freed from any past trauma.[31]

And in all this Holy Spirit, I ask that you be my guide, filling me to overflowing with peace and a greater experience of the love of Christ – not only for myself, but for others too. Amen.

---

[31] See previous footnote

CHAPTER 14
HOME AWAY FROM HOME

One of my greatest childhood memories is of a road trip around Scotland with my grandparents and cousin in a tiny motorhome.

It was the biggest adventure I'd ever been on, and as I was the eldest grandchild I took the lead. I don't think, looking back, that my cousin Steve appreciated my leadership – especially as it involved me pushing him into the icy waters of Loch Lomond (much to my hilarity and his annoyance). However, despite our differences, I know we both revelled in the excitement of the unknown – going to new places, meeting new people and doing new things. We loved the sweeping vistas that appeared around every corner; soaring mountain ranges rising up from deep dark valleys, and purple heather everywhere.

As I recall the details of our trip, what I find interesting is that – even though it was a little scary at times – I always felt secure. Our grandparents were ever present, introducing us to new experiences and encouraging us along the way. Even when the van broke down one rainy evening on a dark back street in Glasgow, there they were with us, sorting it out.

The memories of this trip stand out to me head and shoulders above my other childhood summer holidays. Most of them were spent either on a campsite or in a static caravan in a holiday park with all-age entertainment. This type of holiday resort was fine, except we tended to never leave them. Our holiday experience was restricted to a couple of generic restaurants and a big swimming pool.

Caravan or motorhome?

Which would you choose for a holiday – static caravan or motorhome? Both can be analogies for a life lived with God. Both are meant to be temporary accommodation – a home away from home. This is also true for our lives as humans. We live in a fragile physical body that is wearing out, and will one day break down. Even for those who follow Jesus, this life is a temporary one. The Bible reminds us that we are in the world, but not of it. We are on a journey with the Holy Spirit and our destination is the new heaven and new earth.

You may have heard the expression, "It's all about the journey, not the destination" – but for countless followers of Jesus, once he comes to live in us, we seem to forget about the journey and fix our eyes on where we believe we're going. Other faiths, too, proclaim a future paradise to be enjoyed. For too many years in my life, even before I met Jesus, I lived life for the future. I was always rushing on to the next new thing, the next accomplishment, the next problem. I never took the time to appreciate being in the present. For me as a young mother, that meant focusing on the next developmental milestone in my children's lives – rather than being 'in the moment' with them, simply playing with and enjoying them.

Do you live your life that way? Are you a workaholic, forgetting the privilege of enjoying your own children? Or are you so driven by single-minded pursuits, whether fuelled by fear or passion, that you don't have time to stop and smell the roses?

A well-worn phrase says, "You're too heavenly minded to be any earthly good." It's meant as a chastisement, but I think it misses the point. We *are* to be heavenly minded, but it's about focusing on the 'who', not the 'where' or 'when'. Our focus is to be on the king of heaven, Jesus. Our existence in this life is just like a caravan or motorhome – temporary – but the Holy Spirit encourages us to be fully present in the moment nonetheless – we need to be present to what Jesus is doing here and now. God intends us to experience a taste of heaven now in this life, to see and live his kingdom on earth.

As Christians we can lead very limited lives. We might go to church every Sunday morning, and perhaps – if we're particularly committed – attend a midweek service or a small group of some kind. But those few hours a week can be the extent of our experience of God. In between those meetings our lives can still be focused on the future, the past, our plans, ourselves – anything except for Jesus in the here and now. If we accept that this is all that life in God has to offer, it's like living in a static caravan on a holy all-inclusive holiday resort. We will meet the same people, do the same things, and talk about the same stuff while waiting for our appointed time to travel home to heaven.

This is sad; I believe that many believers are missing out on so much. Jesus offers us much more in the here and now. He died so that we would not only have life, but to live that life to the full (John 10:10).

Are you bored with your life? Do you long for adventure? In my experience, following Jesus isn't boring at all. Since accepting Jesus and inviting him into the 'house' of my life, things have never been the same. His Holy Spirit invites us to go on a journey with him. He calls your temporary home out from inside the confines of the church walls and into the world – with his Spirit compelling and empowering us. That's the difference between a caravan and a motorhome: a caravan has no ability to move itself, while a motorhome has an internal power source that makes it mobile. For a caravan to move it must be hooked up to, or carried by, a vehicle. But we are to be like motorhomes. We are to be empowered by God's Holy Spirit. It is God's internal power in us that enables us to do all the wonderful things he's planned for us and to partner with him in all he has planned to do:

'For we are his workmanship [his own master work, a work of art], created in Christ Jesus [reborn from above—spiritually transformed, renewed, ready to be used] for good works, which God prepared [for us] beforehand [taking paths which he set], so that we would walk in them [living the good life which He prearranged and made ready for us].'

Ephesians 2:10 (AMP)

We are also called to be mobile. That may not mean literally travelling around; but being able to reach out to others beyond ourselves, and outside the safety of the church or house group walls. It's going beyond praying with a Christian friend on a Sunday morning, to offering to pray with a troubled non-Christian colleague on a Monday morning. We were created to do great things. Jesus said, "…whoever believes in me will do the works I have been doing, and they will do even greater things than these, because I am going to the Father" (John 14:12). And what would be greater than healing the sick, casting out demons and raising the dead? We are empowered to do all these things by the engine of the Holy Spirit living inside us. We couldn't do them by our own strength and power – not even with the strongest willpower.

The real church of Jesus Christ has got nothing to do with architecture, but people: Jesus living inside every believer by his Spirit. And we are commanded to move: 'He said to them, "*Go* into all the world and preach the gospel to all creation"' (Mark 16:15).

What does Jesus mean by "Go?" Does that command make you worry about where you should be going? Is God planning to send you on a terrifying journey to a war-torn country? Well, I believe the journey he calls us on is to people, not just to the place where they happen to be. Those people might already be right in front of you.

That's the view of Heidi Baker. It's true that many believers have been called to some of the most difficult places in the world to share the Jesus' good news, and she is one of them. Together with her husband Roland, Heidi leads a ministry called Iris which has thirty-five bases in twenty nations around the world, but is mostly associated with her work in Mozambique caring for orphans and widows. Iris Global feeds tens of thousands daily, has founded thousands of churches and sees the miraculous happening on a regular basis.[32] But Heidi's motto is simply: "Love the one in front of you." Her focus is to love the people she encounters as she travels her life path with Jesus.

---

[32] See www.irisglobal.org. I recommend *Compelled by Love,* a film that documents Heidi Baker's life

Let my people go!

We need to ask Jesus what loving the one in front of you looks like in our own case. The Holy Spirit may lead you to another country as he has lead Keith and I, or just around the streets of your own neighbourhood, perhaps opening your eyes to what you could not see before.

This eye-opening experience has recently happened to our family. Every summer we return to England to attend the New Wine Summer Conference,[33] a week under canvas in the lovely county of Somerset. The event is held over a fortnight, hosting approximately 25,000 thousand Christians who gather to worship Jesus. It's a real family affair, with activities and groups for all ages, as well as international speakers, lots of times of worship and seminars on a whole range of topics. It has become a yearly pilgrimage for us.

We always come with great expectations of hearing from God and being spiritually refreshed, and the summer of 2014 was no different. The Holy Spirit had decided to open our eyes to some of the things that break his heart, and to invite us to move into the work he had planned for us. Danielle Strickland,[34] a serving officer for the Salvation Army in Los Angeles and a gifted, passionate speaker, spoke at one of the evening meetings that we went to. She talked about the Salvation Army's work, both past and present, to rescue those trapped in prostitution and human trafficking. Her talk was inspired by the cry of Moses in Exodus 8:1: "Let my people go!"

Danielle's message was filled with the presence of the Holy Spirit. At the end, she allowed a time of silence for us to sit and reflect on what we'd heard, leaving space for the Holy Spirit to speak. Georgia, our eldest daughter, was sitting with us. Both of our girls have enjoyed their yearly fix of New Wine since they were little, but Georgia hasn't attended church for some years now. In her later teenage years she just couldn't connect to church and its structure, and found being in church and around 'church folk' difficult, so it had been easier for her to stay away. But Jesus had pursued her, continually wooing her back to his love.

---

[33] See https://www.new-wine.org
[34] See Danielle's website www.daniellestrickland.com

So there we sat, together with about 2,000 other people, in silence, waiting on God. Then suddenly Georgia gets to her feet, holds both arms in the air and shouts at the top of her lungs, "Let my people go!" Tears were rolling down her cheeks.

Keith and I turned to look at her, shocked to see that it was our daughter being moved by the Holy Spirit. Before we knew it, other people began to stand too, shouting that same cry of Moses from all those centuries ago. All around the massive tent, men and women stood; we stood too. Thousands of people in unison were crying out for those bound in modern slavery and held captive by the sex trade: "Let my people go!"

All I can say is that we felt the Spirit move that night. The experience changed us. When God moves us like that, he usually has something in store for us to do. The outcome of that encounter with God's Spirit was that Georgia and I now volunteer for Rahab, an outreach to prostitutes in Basel.[35]

What does the Holy Spirit enable us to do when he powers our 'motorhome? Simply put, he enables us to *make a difference*. Staying with the summer holiday theme, I love the following story about a beach. It originated in an essay by American philosopher Loren Eiseley[36] and has been adapted by many over the years; here is my version.

Starfish on the beach

Picture the scene: an expanse of golden beach stretches further than the eye can see below a cloudless azure sky. A little girl and boy walk together, plastic buckets swinging in their hands. The weather today is perfect for making castles in the sand. The sun is shining and the sea is sparkling – but as they get closer to the surf, the sight that greets them is not so beautiful. A great storm has raged in the night, and millions upon millions of little starfish are left stranded on the beach. Unable to get back to the water, they lie on the sand, dying.

The children set to work, gently picking up a starfish each and returning it to the sea. One by one, with the greatest of care, one starfish at a time, back and forth, back and forth, the children work. Sometimes they fill their little buckets

---

[35] See https://www.rahab-basel.ch
[36] Loren Eiseley (1907–1977). See www.eiseley.org

with sea water and walk further up the beach where the sand is dry, where the water rarely reaches. They pick up a starfish and pop it into their little buckets of salty water. They have to walk further to reach the sea but their little buckets are like an oasis in the desert to those starfish – just enough water to revive them until they can be returned home. Trip by trip, bucket by bucket, one starfish after another. The children work with joy, forgetting all about their original plan to build sandcastles.

A man arrives and watches the children at their task.

"What are you doing?" he asks.

"We are helping the starfish get home," says the girl.

"Get home?" the man exclaims. He gestures around at the tragic scene. "Haven't you seen? Don't you realise how many starfish there are here? Millions!"

The children stop working. They look at him and say nothing.

"It's pointless," he says. "Why bother? All your work won't make a bit of difference."

The children smile politely at him, and carry on. They walk to where the waves are lapping against the shore, fill their little buckets once more and walk back up the beach. As the man watches, they pick up, oh so gently, another starfish each and put it in their little reservoirs of life-giving seawater. Then they walk back to the sea and return their starfish to the safety of the water.

The man shakes his head, and turns to walk away.

"Hey, mister!" shouts the boy.

The man looks their way. "What?"

The boy is pointing to the sea, where his starfish has just disappeared under the waves.

"It made a difference to that one, didn't it?"

And the meaning of the story? Well, I guess that the need as we look at the world may seem overwhelming, but if we do what Heidi Baker says and love the one in front of us, we really can make a difference.

Enlarge your tent

Who is God calling you to make a difference to? And if he wants us to go to them, how big is the motorhome you'll be travelling in? Is it a compact minivan, an average-sized motorhome or one of those enormous recreational vehicles (RVs)? In other words, how big is your life?

I'm not talking about how busy you are, the size of your family, or your social status. I mean – how much room have you made for God in your life house?

As babies get older, they grow – and so do we as believers. Although we need to be like children to enter God's kingdom, we are called to grow up spiritually. The more mature we become in our walk with Jesus, the more we expand, to hold more of God. We're like tortoises – the larger their bodies get, the more their shells grow too. God didn't create us to be like hermit crabs, which get too big for their borrowed shells and have to leave them to find a larger one. No, God created us with the capacity to expand and increase. You are unique, and God intends that you grow, with him inside you, to become all that he intended you to be. There is no need to compare ourselves to others or try to recreate another's life as our own. Just as my grandparents accompanied us on that road trip and made me feel secure, God never leaves his children but journeys within each one of us. Moving from motorhomes to tents, remember this:

> '"Enlarge the site of your tent [to make room for more children]; stretch out the curtains of your dwellings, do not spare them; lengthen your tent ropes and make your pegs (stakes) firm [in the ground]. For you will spread out to the right and to the left; and your descendants will take possession of nations and will inhabit deserted cities.'
>
> Isaiah 54: 2–3 (AMP)

We are to grow with God, step by step, room by room, and this is the journey, the adventure on which we embark when we invite Jesus to make his home in our lives. That adventure is being a disciple of Jesus Christ.

In my first year in Switzerland I encountered a very strange sight, though it's one I've got used to now. At certain times of year in this country you can see young men walking the streets who really stand out in a crowd. These (often quite tall) men dress mostly in black, with flared corduroy trousers like hippies from the 1970s. They usually have white shirts and black leather waistcoats, sometimes with long, sweeping coats like great black birds. The ones I saw had unusual hats, some carried a staff or walking stick, and all wore an old-fashioned knapsack. They looked like they'd just walked out of the pages of a fairy tale by the brothers Grimm – or a cross between a Goth and a shepherd.

My neighbour explained that these young men were in fact apprentice carpenters, newly promoted to the rank of 'journeyman'. They leave their hometowns in northern Germany and travel, offering their newly learned carpentry services wherever they go. They only carry with them the tools of their trade. Wherever these men travel, they are to do the good work that they were prepared to do – in their case, carpentry.[37]

So it is for us as followers of Jesus. Just like these journeying carpenters, we should stand out from the crowd, moving wherever God's work takes us, and be known for our good works. We are made to journey but, unlike the young carpenters, our adventure never ends. As children adopted into God's family, even when our physical bodies fail, then our adventure simply begins a new chapter.

And on that note, we'll move onto our final chapter, and a taste of what our heavenly home might be like.

---

[37] Journeymen must work away from home for a minimum of three years and a day, never returning any closer than 50km from their home except in emergencies, such as the death of a relative. They set off with only €5, seeking food and lodging from a network of support contacts. They must not use public transport, only walk or hitch lifts. They must return with no more than the €5 they started with, becoming rich through experience and not money. See www.swissinfo.ch/eng/roving-carpenters-keep-tradition-alive/31454212

RESTORATION REFLECTION

Read the scene below, then close your eyes and ask God to guide your imagination as you picture it. You might find it helpful to write down or draw what you saw in your mind's eye afterwards.

- You are sitting in the driver's seat of your motorhome, ready to set off on a journey, but you don't know where you'll be going. Jesus arrives, and you move across to the passenger seat, inviting him to drive.

    Ask Jesus, "Where do you want to take me? Who can I reach out to?"

    Instead of replying, Jesus starts the engine and the motorhome begins to move. Watch through the windscreen – where, and who, is he taking you to?

TALK TO THE ARCHITECT

Lord Jesus, I sense you calling me to something greater than I am currently experiencing. I long to know you deeper and to really explore this life you have given me but it's so easy for me to fear the unknown and to retreat to the comfort of my normal life. Where I have doubts or a lack of trust, please forgive me Lord.

Holy Spirit, I ask that you expand the horizons of what I think I'm capable of. Come and change my mindset and even my current situation so that I can follow Jesus wherever he leads me. Help me take my place in the great adventure of a life lived for his glory. Amen.

CHAPTER 15
OUR HEAVENLY HOME

Ah, my friend, we are coming to the end of our time together on this journey of restoring your life house. It seems apt, somehow, that I have a sea view as I write this final chapter. I'm sitting on the balcony of our best friend's apartment in Cyprus. We are nearly at the end of what has been two glorious weeks' holiday for Keith and me. It's the first time since our honeymoon twenty-eight years ago that we've had extended holiday time alone together – without our girls, without visiting friends or family, without business meetings or volunteer work to keep us occupied. We've had no agenda or expectations of places to go or things to see. Just time for us. Time to be. Time for God.

There seems to be something inspiring in the Paphos air – perhaps because the apostle Paul preached here, walked this land and saw the same sea, sky and mountains. Or perhaps because yesterday, as I looked out at the view, I couldn't tell where the sea ended and the sky began. As the day went on I felt that this idea – of endless sea and sky – maybe had a deeper, more 'otherworldly' sense to it.

I'm reminded of C. S. Lewis's words in *The Last Battle*, "The term is over: the holidays have begun. The dream is ended: this is the morning."[38] I love the sense of expectation that this evokes in me. Do you remember the feeling you had on the last day of school or university? Lewis was attempting to describe, through the beloved Narnia stories, the end of this life and the beginning of eternity.

---

[38] C. S. Lewis (1956) *The Last Battle*, The Bodley Head. See www.goodreads.com/quotes/70275-the-term-is-over-the-holidays-have

For many of us, these words bring a feeling of relief – but for others perhaps a feeling of apprehension of the unknown. Either way, it speaks of a new reality being revealed. This experience we call life is in fact as fleeting as the blink of an eye or a lover's sigh. It's here one minute and gone the next. But don't worry, my friend – in this life and in the one to come, the same Jesus is in control. And to use the well-known Star Trek misquote, "It's life, Jim, but not as we know it!"[39]

The house of the Lord

Yes, there is a life beyond the one we know, one that is more real than this existence – and one where we are promised eternal life with God through Christ Jesus. The psalmist certainly looked forward to being in 'the house of the Lord':

> 'Surely your goodness and love will follow me all the days of my life, and I will dwell in the house of the LORD forever.'
>
> Psalm 23:6

> 'One thing I ask from the LORD, this only do I seek: that I may dwell in the house of the LORD all the days of my life, to gaze on the beauty of the LORD and to seek him in his temple.'
>
> Psalm 27:4

But what is this house? The Bible offers us a few glimpses. Early on in the history of God's people, Jacob is travelling through the land that will become Israel's. One night God gives him a dream of a staircase with angels walking up and down between heaven and earth. On waking Jacob says, "How awesome is this place! This is none other than the *house of God*; this is the gate of heaven" (Gen 28:17). He renames the place 'Bethel', meaning 'house of

---

[39] This quote is not actually from the Star Trek series, but from a parody song 'Star Trekkin'' released in 1987 by British band The Firm. See https://en.wikipedia.org/wiki/Star_Trekkin'

God' – the first time this word is mentioned in the Bible (Gen 28:19).

Much later the Israelites built a temple in Jerusalem. It contained the ark of the covenant, the gold-covered box that 'housed' the presence of God; it was evidence of God's presence with his people. So the temple became the house of God. Later still, it was Jesus who represented God's presence on earth. He compared his own body to the temple or house of God, saying it would be torn down but that he would build it up again in three days (John 2:19). And now that Jesus is in heaven, it's our bodies that become temples of the Holy Spirit, when we become believers and invite him into our 'life house'.

Of course, none of these houses can actually contain God. Our God is omnipresent – he's everywhere at all times. When King Solomon prayed, after God's presence had filled the new temple, he said, "But will God indeed dwell on the earth? The heavens, even the highest heaven cannot contain you. How much less this temple I have built!" (1 Kings 8:27). This has not stopped most of us, at one time or another, trying to fit God into a box of our own choosing. Sometimes it's the 'Sunday only' box, or the 'religious' box, or reducing God to an old man sitting on a cloud ('Him upstairs', as the English like to call him).

Yet the Bible does tell us of a heavenly home; the place that Jesus promises for those who love him. This is what he comforts us with:

> Do not let your hearts be troubled. You believe in God; believe also in me. My Father's house has many rooms; if that were not so, would I have told you that I am going there to prepare a place for you? And if I go and prepare a place for you, I will come back and take you to be with me that you also may be where I am.
>
> John 14.1–3

So, what will this house of the Father's be like? Apologies if you're expecting to hear about a 'near death experience.' Like most people, I haven't had one. I have to rely on what the Bible says about the eternal home that Jesus has prepared for us.

A vision of heaven

Most of what we are told about heaven is in the final book of the Bible, Revelation – a book of overwhelming imagery and deep mysteries. While I can't claim to fully understand a text that scholars have studied and argued about for centuries, one thing it tells me for sure is that some ideas of heaven out there are false. For a start, heaven is not a place where fat cherubs float around on clouds playing harps all day. Neither is it anything like the Buddhist nirvana, where we lose our individuality and transcend into some kind of soup of cosmic energy. Nor would our God reward any man with ten virgins in his heaven. Heaven, the Bible tells us, is a real place, with structure and form. Revelation talks about a city, coming down from heaven to be on earth. It represents God making his home here on earth with us, joining earth and heaven together forever:

> And I heard a loud voice from the throne saying, "Look! God's dwelling place is now among the people, and he will dwell with them. They will be his people, and God himself will be with them and be their God. He will wipe every tear from their eyes. There will be no more death or mourning or crying or pain, for the old order of things has passed away." He who was seated on the throne said, "I am making everything new!" Then he said, "Write this down, for these words are trustworthy and true."
>
> Revelation 21:3–5

The writer of Revelation, the apostle John, is carried away in the Spirit and shown a brilliant, detailed vision of this new city – a picture of the glory to come:

> It shone with the glory of God, and its brilliance was like that of a very precious jewel, like a jasper, clear as crystal… Then the angel showed me the river of the water of life, as clear as crystal, flowing from the throne of God and of the Lamb down the middle of the great street of the city. On each side of the river stood the tree of

life, bearing twelve crops of fruit, yielding its fruit every month. And the leaves of the tree are for the healing of the nations.

Revelation 21:11; 22:1–2

This glorious vision blows my mind; I love trying to imagine it. No wonder the psalmist declares:

For a day in your courts is better than a thousand [anywhere else];
I would rather stand [as a doorkeeper] at the threshold of the house of my God than to live [at ease] in the tents of wickedness.

Psalm 84:10 (AMP)

Yet, to be entirely honest with you, I still find it hard to get my head around – because I believe it's beyond our ability to fully comprehend right now. We can only compare heaven to what we have conceived with our human minds or what is made by human hands. And despite the Bible telling us that the streets are made with gold, I don't believe heaven will have the gaudy look of a seven-star hotel in Dubai. No, I think it will be breathtakingly beautiful in its elegance and refinement. The imagery used in the *Chronicles of Brothers* book series by the founder of God TV, Wendy Alec, has helped to expand my imagination.[40] She describes beaches made of billions of tiny pearls; a place where the colours are so vivid, it's as if we'd only been seeing things in black and white and now our vision has suddenly been switched to full colour in high definition. It's difficult to believe but yes, something this glorious is to be our reality.

In my research for this chapter, I was surprised to discover that we may even get to build our own houses in God's new heaven and earth: "they will build houses and dwell in them; they will plant vineyards and eat their fruit" (Isa 65. 21). Can you imagine building the house of your dreams, like the ones I mentioned right at the beginning of this book? Not only a house – but our own vineyard too!

---

[40] See www.chroniclesofbrothers.com

My forever life house

So, you might be thinking – what happens to my life house when I am living in eternity? Well, for one thing, it will be complete – all that renovation work finished. And just like at the end of a hard day's work, there will be rest and relaxation. But this is not the end – oh no, my friend, it's just the beginning. You will retire from this life, the one you know now, and you will start afresh. You'll have moved to a new land with Jesus and you won't need to take a single thing from your old life house with you, for Jesus is all you'll ever need. We will all be transformed in the blink of an eye, finally entering fully into who we *really* are.

I'm going to share something with you – something I don't normally tell people lest they think I'm a bit crazy. I believe that *who we are becoming* can break into this world. There's an intriguing verse in Romans that says, "For the creation waits in eager expectation for the children of God to be revealed" (Rom 8:19). What a sight this will be to behold – everyone becoming who they really are as a child of God! But I believe that already, who I will be in eternity is beginning to show itself in me now. I have a feeling that there's somewhere within me an 'inner Mandy' just waiting to break out. Not an alien monster trying to escape, in case you're still thinking about horror films, but the Mandy that God sees – the girl he has always seen. The girl who is complete and perfect, and everything he planned for her to be since before the beginning of time.

This Mandy, the real me, can do lots of things I'm currently unable to do. I sense she's a wonderful ice skater – despite the fact that I have a fear of falling on icy pavements in the winter, and tend to shuffle around on them like an old woman. This Mandy can play classical guitar like a pro – even though my attempts at learning to play ended prematurely when I realised I needed to keep my nails short and that it hurts your fingertips. And lastly, I sense that the new Mandy can ride a horse well – even though, in this reality, I have only ever ridden a donkey on the beach as a child (and you can hardly call that riding; all I did was sit on its back as the guy at the beach led it around a bit). Yet my feeling about the abilities of my 'inner Mandy' are so strong that I have already asked Jesus in prayer if we can go horse riding together one day.

Me on my favourite Palomino mare, and he on a great white stallion, galloping along the shore as the waves of that sea of crystal, like glass, lap on the beach of pearls. And all these things are just a minuscule fraction of the unending possibilities.

It's fun to think about our new physical abilities that lie ahead in the new heaven and earth; but what about all the things Jesus said we would do here and now? Heal the sick, raise the dead, cast out demons and share the good news of Jesus Christ, making disciples of all nations? That's eternity, breaking into our everyday lives. These are the abilities of the people we are becoming, manifesting themselves right now. And not just on Sunday mornings or at special conferences but everywhere we go, every day of our lives this side of eternity. Do you believe that God can do those things through you?

Perhaps it's easier to believe that you can do all these things, and more, if you can sense eternity within you – the real you – the person you are becoming. What does that feel like? What does the real you look like, and what can you do? If you haven't thought about this yet, ask God to show you. Even if you've skipped the reflections at the end of each chapter in this book so far – perhaps you feel that you aren't a reflective kind of person – you might want to give it a go for this final chapter. Take a moment to find out what God wants you to know about the real you. Ask Jesus, and he will break open the heavens and give you a glimpse.

Unfortunately, our time together is coming to an end; so I'll leave you with the reminder that restoring your life house takes time. The new heaven and the new earth will be perfect, but all human attempts at perfection will be at best a pointless task, and at worst a self-imposed prison sentence. As someone who has suffered from obsessive compulsive disorder, I can tell you that attempting a perfect life this side of eternity is a futile activity indeed. On the other hand, if we're sitting comfortably thinking that everything is already just about perfect in our lives, we need to challenge ourselves with this question: Have I sold myself short; have I settled down and accepted that where I am is all there is to experience and achieve? Have I traded my glorious destiny for my own idea of comfort? Jesus living inside our life house will continually call us to be more, to be as he is. It's not that we can live a perfect

Christian life; but as we live in him, the perfection of Christ himself will live in and through us. To this end, Jesus will often revisit every room I've mentioned in our life houses, refining and polishing his workmanship, transforming us from glory to glory.

Here's my encouragement as you continue the restoration work with Jesus:

> We, of course, have plenty of wisdom to pass on to you once you get your feet on firm spiritual ground, but it's not popular wisdom, the fashionable wisdom of high-priced experts that will be out-of-date in a year or so. God's wisdom is something mysterious that goes deep into the interior of his purposes. You don't find it lying around on the surface. It's not the latest message, but more like the oldest—what God determined as the way to bring out his best in us, long before we ever arrived on the scene. The experts of our day haven't a clue about what this eternal plan is. If they had, they wouldn't have killed the Master of the God-designed life on a cross. That's why we have this Scripture text:
> No one's ever seen or heard anything like this,
> Never so much as imagined anything quite like it—
> What God has arranged for those who love him.
> But you've seen and heard it because God by his Spirit has brought it all out into the open before you.
>
> 1 Corinthians 2: 9–10 (MSG)

RESTORATION REFLECTIONS

Choose one of the scenes below, then close your eyes and ask God to guide your imagination as you picture it. You might find it helpful to write down or draw what you saw in your mind's eye afterwards.

- Time has been fast forwarded – you now stand with Jesus on the new earth, in eternity. You are on a building site. Jesus holds in his hands the architect's plans to your dream house, designed especially for you. Ask to see the plans. What does he show you? What kind of house is it? What does it look like? And what does it tell you about the real you who you're becoming?

- How is your journey towards restoration going? Right where you are now, despite knowing all that still needs to change, ask Jesus "How do you see me?" What does he show you? Then ask him, "What room in my life house do you want to work on next?"

TALK TO THE ARCHITECT

Heavenly father, as I wait this side of heaven for Jesus to come and take me home, despite my struggles or suffering, I thank you for this life you have given me.

Lord Jesus I thank you that you came to restore me and that you alone are the key to the door of my eternal home with you.

Holy Spirit I ask that you continue to guide and empower me every day as I take my place in the glorious restoration plans of God. Amen.

APPENDIX – INVITING JESUS

If you want to invite Jesus into your 'life house' and begin a relationship with God, but have trouble finding the words, you can use this simple prayer:

Lord Jesus, I believe you are God's son who came to earth. I believe you lived a sinless life, you died in my place, and you rose again. I believe that you love me and are calling my name. I've heard you knocking on the door of my life, and today I choose to open that door and invite you to live in me.

I'm sorry for the mess I've made. Today I choose to turn away from the wrong choices that have damaged myself or others and separated me from Father God. I ask that you forgive me and help me, as you are the only one who can change me.

I hand over to you the keys of my life house and give you permission to enter every room, restoring my life, changing me from the inside out.

I invite you now, Jesus, to enter my heart by the power of your Holy Spirit. I trust that I will live with you forever.

Amen.

If you have just prayed this for the first time, taking a step of faith into the person and eternal work of Jesus Christ – welcome home! You've joined the family of God himself. All of heaven is delighted, and the adventure begins. The journey with Jesus may not always seem easy, but I can promise you one thing: there will be plenty of joy.

Be brave, and tell someone you trust what you've just done. Then come every day to sit at Jesus' feet in prayer, remembering that God's Spirit is in you. Get yourself a Bible in a modern translation and start reading about all the wonderful things God has done, is doing, and will do. Join a community of people who are having their life houses restored by Jesus too. Begin to take hold of all his promises for you!

As you finish reading this book, I pray that you fully discover the unique and wonderful home that is yours in Jesus' name.

AFTERWORD

So, dear reader, I do hope you've enjoyed our time together. I've certainly enjoyed writing for you and sharing some of my own restoration story. I also hope that my analogy of a 'life house' has helped you see your journey of faith in a practical way – perhaps one that you can access in those hard or dry times when we find it difficult to even get out of bed in the morning, never mind feel God's presence. Remember, we are all works in progress.

The Bible tells us "For it is the Spirit of prophecy who bears testimony to Jesus" (Rev 19:10). It's this power of testimony that can change not only our own lives, but the lives of others, when we share our stories of how Jesus restores us. So I would love to hear your renovation stories, especially if the Holy Spirit has used one of the reflections in this book to reveal more of Jesus and the abundant life he continuously offers.

As a final encouragement, I will leave you with these words:

> I am convinced and confident of this very thing, that He who has begun a good work in you will [continue to] perfect and complete it until the day of Christ Jesus [the time of His return].
>
> Philippians 1:6 (AMP)

ABOUT THE AUTHOR

Mandy was born and grew up in England, but has lived in Switzerland since 2001 with her husband Keith and two daughters. With Keith, she is part of the leadership team at Oikos International Church in Basel. Keith and Mandy have ministered together as a couple for many years leading and training Alpha courses, and developed and run the course, 'Growing sexual intimacy in marriage'. Most recently Mandy has been working as a home organisation consultant and coach.

Mandy's other roles include:
- Speaker ambassador for Compassion Switzerland, a Christian child sponsorship charity; she and Keith sponsor three children
- Volunteer with Rahab, a Salvation Army outreach to sex workers in Basel's red-light district.
- Leader at the Saphira women's ministry in Basel, speaking at regular events for this and at other churches in Switzerland.

Her debut book was *Gorgeous: Seeing yourself through God's eyes* (Evangelista Media, 2014). It was published in German as *'Du bist wünderschon: Mit den Augen Gottes sehen'* (Cap Books, 2014).

Mandy loves to encourage others and demonstrate how a relationship with Jesus Christ changes our lives, here and now. She is passionate about sharing the treasurers and freedoms of following Jesus, and delights to help people on their journey to become all that God intended them to be, by sharing her own life story with refreshing honesty and down-to-earth humour. Her motivation is simply this: "Come and hear, all you who fear God; let me tell you what he has done for me" (Psalm 66:16).

You may contact Mandy Muckett at:

Email: info@mandymuckett.com
Website: www.mandymuckett.com
Facebook Page: Mandy Muckett – Author and Speaker
Twitter Account: @MandyMuckett

Printed in Poland
by Amazon Fulfillment
Poland Sp. z o.o., Wrocław